Plant Ecology

The Green World

Forestry

Photosynthesis and Respiration

Plant Cells and Tissues

Plant Development

Plant Ecology

Plant Genetics

Plant Nutrition

Plant Ecology

J. Phil Gibson and
Terri R. Gibson

CHELSEA HOUSE
PUBLISHERS
An imprint of Infobase Publishing

Plant Ecology

Copyright © 2006 by Infobase Publishing

Chelsea House
An imprint of Infobase Publishing
132 West 31st Street
New York NY 10001

Library of Congress Cataloging-in-Publication Data

Gibson, J. Phil.
    Plant ecology/J.Phil Gibson and Terri R. Gibson
        p. cm. — (The green world)
    Includes bibliographical references.
    ISBN: 0-7910-8566-X
    1. Plant ecology—Juvenile literature. I. Gibson, Terri R. II. Title. III. Series.
QK901.G53 2006
581.7—dc22   2005019381

Text design by Keith Trego
Cover design by Keith Trego
Composition by 21st Century Publishing and Communications, Inc.
Cover printed by IBT Global, Troy, NY
Book printed and bound by IBT Global, Troy, NY
Date printed: December 2009
Printed in the United States of America

10 9 8 7 6 5 4 3

This book is printed on acid-free paper.

Table of Contents

Introduction

By William G. Hopkins

"Have you thanked a green plant today?" reads a popular bumper sticker. Indeed we should thank green plants for providing the food we eat, fiber for the clothing we wear, wood for building our houses, and the oxygen we breathe. Without plants, humans and other animals simply could not exist. Psychologists tell us that plants also provide a sense of well-being and peace of mind, which is why we preserve forested parks in our cities, surround our homes with gardens, and install plants and flowers in our homes and workplaces. Gifts of flowers are the most popular way to acknowledge weddings, funerals, and other events of passage. Gardening is one of the fastest growing hobbies in North America and the production of ornamental plants contributes billions of dollars annually to the economy.

Human history has been strongly influenced by plants. The rise of agriculture in the fertile crescent of Mesopotamia brought previously scattered hunter-gatherers together into villages. Ever since, the availability of land and water for cultivating plants has been a major factor in determining the location of human settlements. World exploration and discovery was driven by the search for herbs and spices. The cultivation of new world crops—sugar, cotton, and tobacco—was responsible for the introduction of slavery to America, the human and social consequences of which are still with us. The push westward by English colonists into the rich lands of the Ohio River Valley in the mid-1700s was driven by the need to increase corn production and was a factor in precipitating the French and Indian War. The Irish Potato Famine in 1847 set in motion a wave of migration, mostly to North America, that would reduce the population of Ireland by half over the next 50 years.

As a young university instructor directing biology tutorials in a classroom that looked out over a wooded area, I would ask each group of students to look out the window and tell me what they saw. More often than not the question would be met with a blank, questioning look. Plants are so much a part of our environment and the fabric of our everyday lives that they rarely register in our conscious thought. Yet today, faced with disappearing rainforests, exploding population growth, urban sprawl, and concerns about climate change, the productive capacity of global agricultural and forestry ecosystems is put under increasing pressure. Understanding plants is even more essential as we attempt to build a sustainable environment for the future.

THE GREEN WORLD series opens doors to the world of plants. The series describes what plants are, what plants do, and where plants fit into the overall scheme of things. *Plant Ecology* explores ecological roles and dynamics of plants in their environment, highlighting important concepts ranging from individual plant interactions to entire ecosystems.

1 Plants and the Environment

Study nature, love nature, stay close to nature.
It will never fail you.

— Frank Lloyd Wright

Plants and the Environment

The tallgrass prairies of North America are excellent examples of the dynamic relationship between plants and their environment. At first, prairies might appear to be a sea of grass, no different from a lawn except for the height of the plants. However, closer inspection reveals that this is not the case. Different grasses, such as big bluestem, switchgrass, Indian grass, and little bluestem, clearly dominate the landscape, but there are also plants such as ironweed, sunflowers, compass plant, milkweeds, and many others mixed in among the grasses. Some species occur as individual plants scattered across the landscape, while others occur in distinct clusters (Figure 1.1).

The distribution and growth of plants in the prairie is affected by numerous living (**biotic**) and nonliving (**abiotic**) factors (Table 1.1). For example, moist locations along streams and ponds support the growth of trees such as cottonwood and willow. Dry locations, however, cannot support tree growth because the grasses (with their fibrous root systems just below the soil surface) quickly take up what little water is available. Recently burned areas in the prairie support the dense growth of herbs and grasses because fire enhances nutrient availability in the soil. Bison prefer to graze in recently burned areas because the grasses there are more nutritious. Bison grazing "trims back" the dominant grasses, allowing other plants to establish and grow. Bison urine and dung further enhance nutrient availability in the soil, which supports the growth of some plants and suppresses the

Table 1.1 Biotic and Abiotic Components of the Environment

Biotic	Plants of the same species, plants of different species, animals, fungi, bacteria
Abiotic	Temperature, sunlight, water, soil nutrients, topography

Figure 1.1 The tallgrass prairies of North America contain different species of plants (including grasses, ironweed, sunflowers, and compass plants) and animals (such as bison) interacting with their environment to form a dynamic ecosystem.

growth of others. These phenomena and many others are all part of a functioning **ecosystem** (Figure 1.2). Ecosystems are composed of populations of different **species** that live in an area, as well as the nonliving components of the environment such as temperature, water availability, and sunlight.

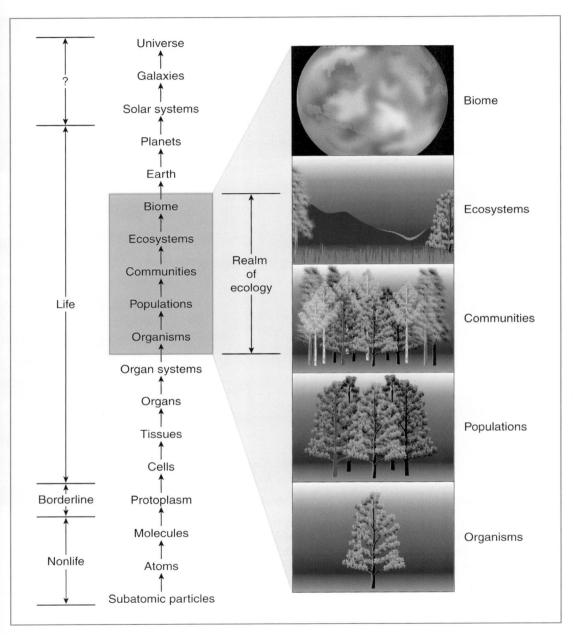

Figure 1.2 The realm of ecology spans five levels in biological organization. Plant ecology studies the relationships and interactions between plants and their environment, from the level of individual plants to large geographic ecosystems (biomes).

Plants are the foundation of ecosystems. Through **photosynthesis,** energy in sunlight is converted into sugars or other carbohydrates that plants use as an energy source. Plants also play a vital role in cycling nutrients through ecosystems. Nitrogen, phosphorus, potassium, and other essential nutrients dissolved in soil water are taken up by plant roots and incorporated into plant tissue. Other organisms consume plants to acquire the energy and nutrients they need to survive.

Beyond playing a critical role in energy flow and nutrient cycling, plants interact with and impact their **environment** in many other ways. Their presence provides not only food but also **habitat** for other organisms. Plants influence temperature and other aspects of **climate**. They also compete with one another for resources in the environment. These and many other phenomena demonstrate that plants are not just a passive backdrop on the landscape, but are a dynamic part of their environment.

Plant ecology is the discipline within the larger field of **ecology** that investigates the relationships and interactions between plants and their environment (see "Diversity of Plant Life" box). The term *ecology* was coined in 1869 by German biologist Ernst Haeckel. His term, *oekologie*, a combination of the Greek roots *oikis* ("the home") and *logos* ("the study of"), means the study of organisms in their home or environment. Environment encompasses everything that can influence or be influenced by an organism, including biotic factors (other living organisms) and abiotic factors such as temperature, water availability, and soil.

Modern plant ecologists investigate a wide variety of topics and utilize a diversity of scientific methods. Some researchers combine modern satellite imagery with on-site inventories of plant species to study patterns of vegetation organization and change on the landscape. Other plant ecologists combine genetic analyses with field studies to determine how plant reproductive traits shape patterns of pollen and seed dispersal in plant populations. Still

Diversity of Plant Life

There are over 300,000 different species of plants. Scientists organize species into four groups. **Bryophytes** are the oldest group, evolving over 430 million years ago. They include over 20,600 species of mosses, liverworts, hornworts, and quillworts. Bryophytes lack **vascular tissue** and depend on diffusion for uptake of water and minerals from the soil and distribution of those materials throughout the plant. They are small and typically live in moist habitats.

A second group, **ferns and fern allies**, includes true ferns, whisk ferns, horsetails, and club mosses. These plants evolved over 420 million years ago. There are over 13,000 species in this group, most of them ferns. Like bryophytes, ferns and fern allies reproduce via spores, but they have vascular tissues that transport water and nutrients around the plant body and provide structural support for the plant.

Gymnosperms include plants such as junipers, pines, ginkgos, and cycads. They have vascular tissue and produce cones containing seeds or pollen for reproduction. Vascular tissue in gymnosperms can develop into wood to transport water and provide tremendous strength to the plant body. The first gymnosperms evolved over 360 million years ago. Although very diverse in the past, there are presently only 720 gymnosperm species.

Angiosperms, the flowering plants, are currently the most diverse group with over 250,000 species. Like gymnosperms, they are vascular and produce seeds. However, rather than cones, angiosperms use **flowers** and fruits for reproduction. Angiosperms evolved over 125 million years ago. The ecological benefits of flowers and fruits promoted the rapid diversification of angiosperms, leading to their present dominance of Earth.

Although they are not plants, **fungi** and **lichens** are important in plant ecology. Fungi obtain their food by secreting digestive enzymes on living or dead organisms and then absorbing the organic molecules. Lichens are symbiotic organisms composed of a fungus and a green alga or cyanobacterium.

others conduct detailed biochemical analyses to investigate how some plant species have evolved defenses to repel animals that might attempt to eat their leaves. Although these research topics and techniques are very different from one another, they all seek to understand the many ways that plants interact with and shape their environment.

PLANT ADAPTATIONS

A central principle of ecology is that organisms must have traits which help them fit and survive in their environment. For example, a cactus produces shallow roots that allow it to rapidly absorb any rainfall in the desert and specialized cells in its stem that swell to store that water. Instead of conducting photosynthesis, the leaves are modified into spines that protect the cactus from animals that may try to eat it. Photosynthesis occurs in the outer layers of its succulent, green stem.

The traits of the cactus described above are its **phenotype**, which is any structural, biochemical, or behavioral characteristic expressed by an organism. The genes in the DNA that code for the phenotype are the **genotype**. Genetically based phenotypic traits that promote survival and reproductive success of an organism in its environment are **adaptations**. For example, the shallow roots, photosynthetic stems, and spines are adaptations that promote cactus survival in the desert.

However, the phenotype is not controlled by genes alone. Plants may also adjust their phenotypes in response to local environmental conditions (Figure 1.3). For example, genes control the shape and structure of leaves for a species. When a plant grows in shaded conditions, its leaves will be larger and thinner than leaves on a plant grown in full sunlight. The leaves of the sun-grown plant may also produce hairs on the leaf surface to reflect some of the light, whereas the leaf on a shade-grown plant will be darker to help it absorb more light. Such modification of the phenotype due to the environment is called **phenotypic plasticity**.

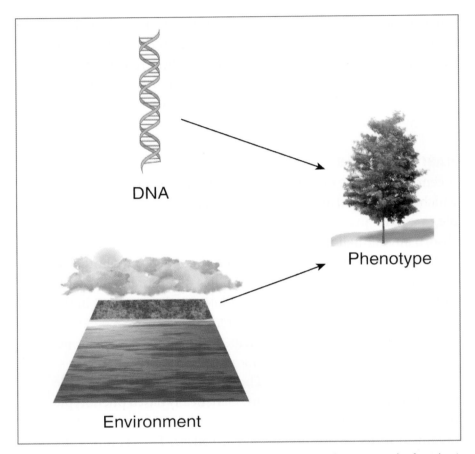

DNA

Phenotype

Environment

Figure 1.3 The structure, biochemistry, and behavior (phenotype) of a plant result from its genes as well as its adaptation to the local environment. Plants may adjust their phenotypes in response to local environments.

Through plasticity, individual plants can make adjustments of form and function to fit their particular environmental conditions. Plasticity is a short-term change of phenotype by an individual in response to its environment, whereas adaptations are long-term changes of phenotype in response to environment that are passed from parent to offspring.

Adaptations occur through the process of evolution. Evolution is a change in the frequency of genetically based characteristics

in a species over time. The mechanism of evolution that promotes the spread of adaptations in a species and increases the
fit between organisms and their environment is **natural selection**
(see "Natural Selection: Darwin & Wallace" box). Natural
selection occurs when organisms with certain phenotypes have

Natural Selection: Darwin & Wallace

The discovery of natural selection involves one of the most intriguing coincidences in the history of biology. In 1858, Charles Darwin was in England developing his theory of evolution by natural selection based upon observations made while traveling on the *H.M.S. Beagle.* At the same time, Alfred Wallace was independently developing a similar theory while conducting field work in the Malay Archipelago. Wallace sent a manuscript outlining his theory to Darwin and asked him to pass it on to members of the scientific community in London. After reading Wallace's manuscript, Darwin was dumbfounded by the similarity to his own work. He presented both manuscripts to a group of scientists in London, the Linnean Society.

Both authors highlighted the importance of variation in characteristics among members of the same species. For example, farmers selectively breed individuals (**artificial selection**) to increase the occurrence of desirable traits in livestock or crops. Darwin and Wallace concluded that the same process occurs in nature, where individuals with traits better suited to their particular environment will secure more resources and leave more descendents over time. Favorable traits will spread which can change species' characteristics and even give rise to new species.

For a variety of reasons, Darwin's theory, as published in *The Origin of Species,* would be the one widely accepted in the scientific community. Although not as well known for the discovery of natural selection, Wallace continued his work and made major contributions to the field of plant biogeography.

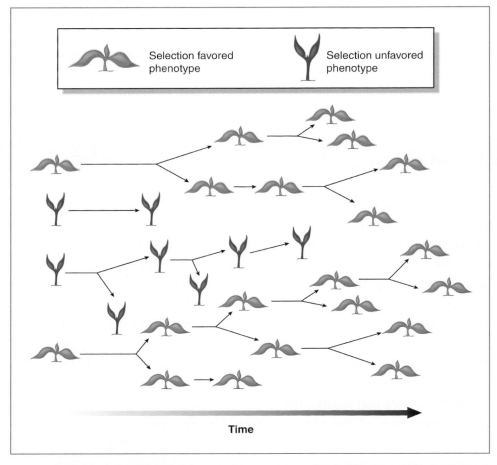

Figure 1.4 Natural selection favors plants with traits (phenotypes) that enhance survival or produce more offspring. Over time, those genes for the favored traits will be passed on and become more common in successive generations.

either greater survival or produce more offspring in a particular environment than organisms with other phenotypes. Because the more successful phenotypic trait is controlled by genes, those genes will be passed on and the adaptive traits will become more prevalent in future generations (Figure 1.4). It is important to note, however, that if environmental conditions change, the value of a particular phenotype can change as well.

ECOTYPES

Although members of a species are highly similar, **populations** can become adapted to the particular set of environmental conditions where they grow (see "Metal Tolerance and Local Adaptation" box). These locally adapted forms of a species are called **ecotypes**.

Experiments on yarrow and sticky cinquefoil provide classic examples of ecotypic differentiation. Both species grow in locations that range from sea level to near the tops of the Sierra Nevada Mountains in California. Plants from lower elevations are taller and more robust than plants growing at higher

Metal Tolerance and Local Adaptation

Heavy metals such as zinc, lead, mercury, and copper can be toxic to plants, even if they occur at low levels in the soil. Areas with naturally high levels of heavy metals in the soil often support distinctive assemblages of plant species that have evolved special tolerance to the toxic conditions in these soils. However, species which normally could not survive in high-metal soils have been found growing in toxic locations such as mine tailing heaps that are contaminated with heavy metals.

Researchers have investigated whether heavy metal tolerance is an inherent characteristic of a species or whether the plants have evolved tolerant ecotypes. In these experiments, plants from both high- and low-metal soils are grown under high-metal conditions. For inherently tolerant species, such as alpine pennycress, plants from low- and high-metal soils grow equally well in the presence of high metals in the soil. In species with evolved tolerance, such as switchgrass, plants from high-metal sites grow under high- and low-metal conditions, but plants from low-metal sites die when exposed to high heavy metals. The plants that have evolved metal tolerance often grow within meters of non-tolerant individuals, which indicates that soil contamination can provide sufficient environmental pressure for natural selection to cause adaptations even over short distances.

elevations, with plants from mid-elevation populations being the tallest of all (Figure 1.5). These differences are related to environmental variation among sites. For example, the short growing season and lower temperature found at high elevations favors smaller plants that can complete their life cycle rapidly and tolerate freezing temperatures and high snowfall. Lower elevation sites have a much longer growing season, experience warmer temperatures, and receive more rain, which allows plants to grow for a longer period and achieve larger size.

To determine whether these differences in form are due to **acclimation,** in which the plants adjust their growth or physiology in response to local conditions, or adaptation, researchers collected seeds from plants at different elevations and grew them at sea level. The plants that grew from these seeds continued to express differences in height, flowering, and other traits that reflected the characteristics of their population of origin (i.e., seeds collected from high elevations produced smaller plants while seeds collected from low elevations produced taller plants, regardless of where the researchers grew them). Likewise, when plants from given elevations were grown at other elevations, the plants did not grow or survive as well as they did at the elevation from which they were collected. The experiment showed that although plant phenotypes were partly influenced by local growing conditions, the differences in growth form among populations were primarily due to genetic adaptations to a given locality. These studies demonstrate how natural selection can cause populations of wide-ranging species to genetically diverge from one another and become adapted to their unique environmental conditions.

Summary
Plant ecology is the scientific study of plants and their environment. Plants have unique traits, such as photosynthesis, that

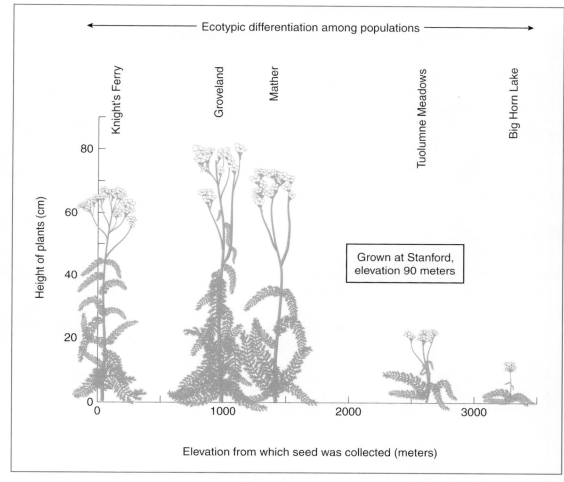

Figure 1.5 Populations of plants adapt to their local environment, sometimes leading to starkly different forms (ecotypes) even within a species. Here, yarrow plant ecotypes from lower elevations grow much taller than those at higher elevations.

dictate how they function in and interact with their environment. Plant diversity is organized into different taxonomic groups, with species being the fundamental unit. Different species of plants have adaptations that help them survive in their home environment. Within species, populations can also become adapted to the distinct conditions of their local environment.

2 Life Cycles and Life History

The Breath becomes a stone; the stone, a plant; the plant, an animal; the animal, a man; the man, a spirit; and the spirit, a god.

— Christian Nestell Bovee

Life Cycles and Life History

Bristlecone pine is the ultimate long-lived species. A bristlecone pine population in the White Mountains of California contains the oldest living organisms on Earth. Many trees are over 1,000 years old and several have been aged at over 4,700 years old (the seeds for these plants germinated before the pyramids were built). Bristlecone pines grow slowly, less than 1/100th of an inch in diameter per year. Individual leaves are retained on the tree for 20–30 years. After growing for many years, trees become reproductively mature and begin producing seeds. Incredibly slow growth and investment of resources toward survival of the individual allow bristlecone pines to achieve their ancient age.

Pool sprite, in contrast, rarely lives longer than three to four weeks. It grows in depressions on granite rock outcrops in the southeastern United States. Water gathers in the depressions during spring rains in March and April. The correct water and temperature conditions in these pools stimulate germination of dormant pool sprite seeds in the thin soil layer at the bottom of the depressions. Plants quickly grow to approximately 6 mm (0.234 inches) in height, flower, set seed, and die, completing their entire life cycle before the pool dries and becomes unsuitable for growth until the following year. Rather than allocating resources toward longevity, pool sprite directs its efforts towards rapid growth and speedy reproduction to survive in its ephemeral environment.

Although bristlecone pine and pool sprite are extremely different species, they both exhibit the same general life cycle pattern of plants. First, the seed germinates, followed by a period of seedling growth. Next, the juvenile plant grows and becomes reproductively mature. Then, after producing offspring once or many times, the plant enters a post-reproductive period and eventually dies.

The collective life cycle and reproductive characteristics of a species that influence survival and the production of offspring are called the **life history**. This includes traits such as life span, frequency of reproduction, and number of offspring produced. Because resources are limited, life history traits are often viewed as trade-offs among competing demands for resources. For example, energy resources within the individual can be allocated either to the growth of the individual plant or to the production of offspring. Likewise, energy resources for reproduction can be divided among either many, smaller offspring or fewer, larger offspring. Natural selection favors combinations of life history traits that maximize the production and survival of offspring. Because of this, certain combinations of life history traits provide more successful strategies for survival than others in particular environments.

LIFE SPAN

A fundamental plant life history characteristic is life span. **Annuals** are **herbaceous** plants that complete their life cycle within one year (Figure 2.1). This process can occur over many months or over a matter of weeks. In contrast, **perennials** are plants that live two years or more. Some herbaceous perennials store nutrients in underground structures such as **bulbs, rhizomes, tubers** or **corms** which they use to produce new herbaceous foliage above ground each year. Other perennials, such as shrubs and trees, produce wood in stems, branches, and roots. Leaves on woody perennials may die back when conditions are unfavorable, but the aboveground woody tissues persist.

PLANT GROWTH

Plants differ from other organisms in terms of how they grow. Plant growth is restricted to localized regions called **meristems** (Figure 2.2). Meristems are found at the growing tips of stems (**shoot apical meristem**) or roots (**root apical meristem**) and contribute to elongation of the plant. Another meristem, the **vascular cambium**, causes increases in stem diameter through the production of wood in shrubs and trees (see "Big Trees" box).

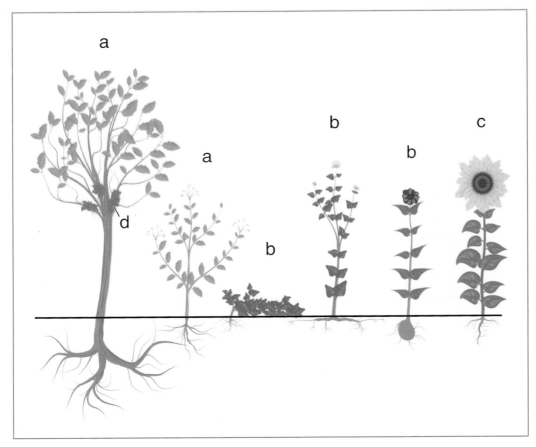

Figure 2.1 Life span is a fundamental plant life history characteristic. Woody (a) and herbaceous (b) perennials live two years or more. The herbaceous annual (c) completes its life cycle in one year. Epiphytes (d) are non-parasitic plants that grow on trees.

Meristems in perennials respond to the environment by growing when conditions are favorable and going dormant when conditions are unfavorable for growth. This behavior causes the vascular cambium to produce **growth rings** in the wood of temperate species. Researchers extract wood cores from tree trunks to count the growth rings and age trees (Figure 2.3). Plant ecologists analyze the size of growth rings to determine patterns of growth and environmental conditions in the past.

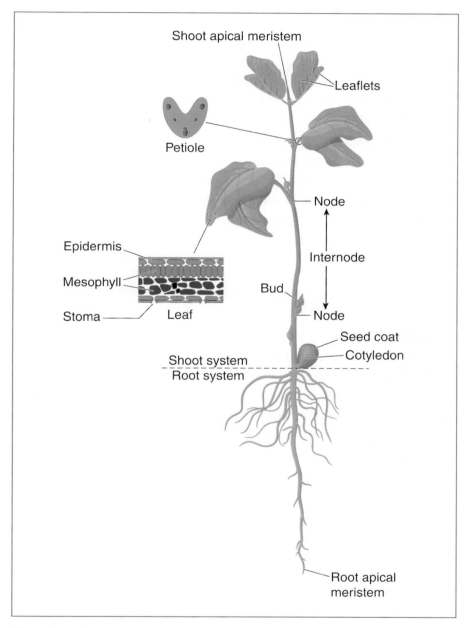

Figure 2.2 Growth in plants is restricted to localized regions called meristems, which are found at the tips of stems (shoot apical meristem) and roots (root apical meristem).

EVERGREEN VS. DECIDUOUS

Woody perennial species are often characterized based upon whether they shed or retain their leaves throughout the year. **Evergreen** plants retain functional leaves on the plant throughout the year. Many common evergreens, such as pines, spruce, and fir, thrive in extremely cold regions, but species in tropical rain forests are also evergreen due to the year round growing season. **Deciduous** species drop their leaves when conditions become unfavorable for plant growth. Temperate region trees and shrubs, such as oaks, maples, and hickories, shed their leaves in the fall. Some tropical plants may shed their leaves prior to the onset of the dry season. Desert species, such as

Big Trees

Depending on how one defines size, there are individuals in several different species that can rightfully claim the title of the largest organism on Earth. The tallest tree species is the coast redwood. The tallest coast redwood, named the Mendocino Tree, grows in the Sierra Nevada Mountains of coastal California. Its trunk stands a towering 112 meters (367 feet) tall and is over 3,200 years old. The second tallest species, which also grows in California, is the giant sequoia, whose largest member (nicknamed General Sherman) is 84 meters (276 feet) tall and over 3,500 years old. The tree with the largest diameter is a chestnut growing on Mount Etna in Sicily named "The Tree of One Hundred Horses." It has a diameter of over 58 meters (190 feet). If size is based on area, the largest tree in the world is a quaking aspen **clone** named Pando (meaning "I spread") in the Wasatch Mountains of Utah. It is composed of approximately 47,000 trunks covering over 43 hectares (106 acres). This clone may be over 10,000 years old. Pando has achieved its tremendous size producing trunks called suckers that originate from underground roots to form a new trunk and promote spread of the clone.

Figure 2.3 Growth in temperate trees increases the vascular cambium, adding wood to the trunk diameter in growth rings. These growth rings can be used to measure the age of the tree.

devil's walking stick, also drop their leaves when conditions become dry.

A common misconception is that the terms *evergreen* and *deciduous* are synonymous with *gymnosperm* and *angiosperm*, respectively. This is not the case. While many gymnosperms are indeed evergreen, species such as ginkgo, bald cypress, and larch are deciduous. Likewise, there are evergreen angiosperms, such as magnolia, azalea, and holly, that do not shed their leaves during the winter.

Evergreen and deciduous plants allocate resources in leaves differently. Evergreen species invest energy to produce thick cell walls and other features that enable their leaves to withstand a range of environmental conditions over several years. Deciduous species on the other hand, do not invest as much energy toward strengthening leaves because their leaves must function for only a single growing season.

FREQUENCY OF REPRODUCTION

The number of times an organism will reproduce is a very important life history trait that reflects trade-offs in energy allocation between the parent's survival and the production of offspring (see "Male and Female Function in Angiosperms" box). Some species are **semelparous,** producing offspring once during their lifetime. Other species are **iteroparous,** producing offspring many times over the life of the individual.

All annual plants are semelparous. Initially, they allocate their energy resources to stem, leaf, and root production. Later, resource allocation shifts to the production of reproductive structures such as flowers, fruits, and seeds. Because the individual plant will die after reproducing, there is no further allocation toward growth and maintenance of the plant body.

Not all semelparous species are annuals. Perennial species, such as the century plant, grow in the desert for many years accumulating energy resources and storing them in the roots (Figure 2.4). When the plant has achieved sufficient size and environmental cues indicate the appropriate conditions for reproduction, the plant uses the stored energy to produce a large structure containing many flowers. The plant expends all of its stored resources in this "big bang" reproductive event and then dies. This strategy is successfully used by many desert species for two reasons. First, due to harsh desert conditions, it may take many years for an individual plant to establish itself and acquire sufficient resources for reproduction. Second, the right conditions for germination

Figure 2.4 The century plant is a perennial semelparous plant. This plant spends years accumulating enough energy to produce flowers and reproduce before dying.

of seeds are variable and unpredictable. Yearly production of seeds in these desert perennials would cause valuable resources to be wasted on producing offspring that would have no chance of survival.

Many perennials are iteroparous. As with annuals, resources are initially directed toward growth and establishment of the young plant. Once sufficient size has been reached, the plant begins allocating resources toward reproduction. Because the plant will live on after it has reproduced, perennials must balance

Male and Female Function in Angiosperms

Unlike most animals, in which males and females are separate individuals, flowers are typically **hermaphroditic**, containing both male and female structures in the same flowers. Over 72% of angiosperm species are hermaphroditic, while only 10% produce separate male and female plants (**dioecy**). The remaining 18% have a variety of other gender combinations such as **monoecy** (separate male and female flowers on the same plant) and **gynodioecy** (some plants produce hermaphroditic flowers and others produce female flowers). Hermaphroditism is valuable to a plant because it allows a plant to reproduce by mating with itself and it provides the opportunity for reproductive success through both male (pollen) and female (seed) functions.

Given the value of hermaphroditism, ecologists have asked why these other gender systems that involve loss of either male or female function in some plants would evolve. These studies have identified several answers to this question. First, being unisexual promotes mating between different individuals. Hermaphroditic plants may self-fertilize, which can cause inbreeding and reduced viability in offspring. Second, unisexual plants can specialize how they allocate resources for reproduction. Because male and female function can place conflicting resource demands on a plant, a unisexual plant can allocate all resources toward reproductive success as male or female.

resource allocation between reproduction and continued growth and maintenance of the adult plant.

LIFE HISTORY STRATEGIES

Some combinations of life history traits tend to be more common than others. These combinations can be thought of as successful strategies for individual survival and reproduction. Ecologists have developed different systems to categorize these different strategies. One system characterizes plants as being either **r-strategists** or **K-strategists** (Table 2.1). In r-strategists (r is the variable for rate

Table 2.1 Life History Traits of r-strategy and K-strategy Plants

	r	K
Habitat	Variable, unpredictable	Constant, stable
Population size	Variable, recolonization frequent, often below carrying capacity	Fairly constant and close to carrying capacity
Survival of the individual plant	Individual plants tend to live full life span for species	Most plants die young, few live full life span possible for the species
Life span	Relatively short	Long
Mortality	Catastrophic, unpredictable, independent of population density	Predictable, often related to population density
Reproduction	Semelparous, high seed production	Iteroparous
Natural selection favors	Rapid growth, early reproduction, small size, early maturity	Slow growth, built to last, late reproduction, large size
Examples	Annuals, weeds	Perennials, trees, shrubs

of population increase in mathematical models of population growth), natural selection favors traits such as rapid maturation and the production of many offspring in a single reproductive event. This combination of traits promotes rapid population growth. Dandelions and other so-called **weeds** are examples of r-strategists (see "What is a Weed?" box).

In K-strategists (K is the variable for **carrying capacity**, which is the maximum size of a population that can survive in an area),

What Is a Weed?

Everyone knows a weed when they see it. Weeds are the plants that nobody wants to grow. When most people talk about weeds, they mean a plant growing where it is not wanted. Any plant could meet this simple criterion, but most often the term *weed* is used for undesirable, problematic plants such as crabgrass, thistle, or dogbane that invade gardens, lawns, or fields and must be manually removed or chemically suppressed. Though their names are often less than complementary, some of these weeds are beautiful wildflowers.

When botanists and plant ecologists speak of weeds, they are referring to plants that have a particular set of life history characteristics. In general, weeds are opportunistic species that predominantly grow in areas disturbed by humans. They grow flowers quickly and produce many seeds that can germinate over a wide range of conditions. These traits allow weed populations to grow rapidly. Because weeds must constantly colonize new areas, they often have adaptations that promote long-distance seed dispersal. Although weeds may be removed above ground, their seeds can remain dormant in the soil for many years, waiting until conditions are right to germinate. Some weeds have large roots that are firmly anchored to the ground. Even with the stem removed, the root can resprout and produce another plant. Weeds are also strong competitors. They grow quickly and take up water and other resources faster than other plants. Although gardeners may have little use for weeds, scientists find them invaluable in the study of plant life history and evolution.

natural selection favors traits that promote survival in stable populations that are near or at carrying capacity. K-strategists are typically long-lived perennials that grow slowly and reproduce many times over the life of an individual. Many forest trees are K-strategists.

A different model, which more accurately represents the strategies in plants, differentiates three different strategies: R, C, and S (Figure 2.5, Table 2.2). The R strategy is used by **ruderals**, annuals that live in areas in which the vegetation is disturbed, but there are ample resources available. The C strategy is used by competitive species that live in stable environments in which there is little disturbance but ample resources. Individuals with this strategy have rapid growth and are strong competitors for resources in the environment. The S strategy is used by stress-tolerant species. These plants grow slowly in harsh but stable environments in which there are few resources available. Annuals and weeds are typical R-strategists. Trees and shrubs tend to be C- and S-strategists. Lichens and desert plants are S-strategists.

Summary

The life history of a species includes the various strategies that plants use to survive and reproduce during their life cycles. Life history traits reflect tradeoffs between conflicting demands on limited resources within an individual. The way in which a species combines these traits enables it to fit particular environmental conditions. One life history model characterizes plants as either rapid growing r-strategists or more slow growing K-strategists. A different model groups plants into one of three different strategies: ruderal, competitive, or stress tolerant. These life history models highlight how natural selection favors certain combinations of traits that allow individuals to survive and successfully reproduce in their environment.

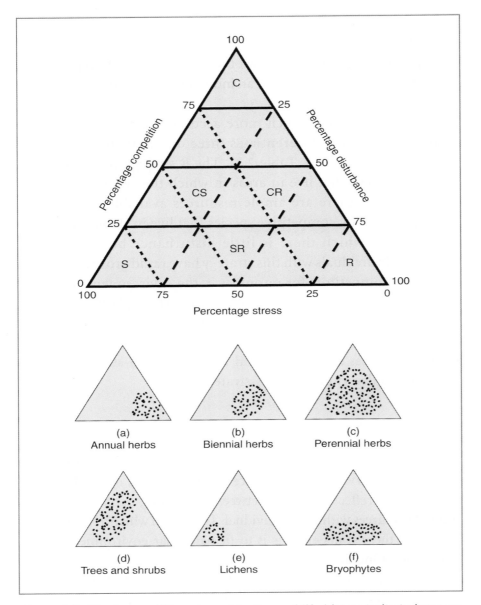

Figure 2.5 Plants use different combinations of life history traits to increase survival. The Ruderal (R) strategy is used by plants that grow in disturbed areas with ample resources. The Competitive (C) strategy is used by competitive species that grow rapidly in stable environments. The Stress (S) strategy involves stress-tolerant species that grow in harsh environments.

Table 2.2 Life History Traits of Plants with Ruderal (R), Competitive (C), and Stress Tolerant (S) Strategies

	R	C	S
Habitat	Variable, unpredictable	Constant, stable	Constant, extreme hot or cold, low nutrient availability
Population size	Variable, recolonization frequent, often below carrying capacity	Fairly constant and close to carrying capacity	Fairly constant and close to carrying capacity
Survival of the individual plant	Plants tend to live full life span for species	Most plants die young, few live full life span possible for the species	Most plants die young, few live full life span possible for the species
Life span	Relatively short	Short or long	Long
Mortality	Catastrophic, unpredictable, independent of population density	Predictable, often related to population density	Predictable, often related to population density
Reproduction	Semelparous, high seed production	Iteroparous, relatively low seed production	Iteroparous, infrequent and only when conditions are favorable
Natural selection favors	Rapid growth, early reproduction, small size	Rapid growth, early reproduction, large size, strong competitors	Slow growth, built to last, late reproduction, large size, high tolerance of stressful conditions
Examples	Annual herbs	Perennial herbs, shrubs, and trees	Perennial herbs, shrubs, trees, and lichens

The goal of life is living in agreement with nature.

— Zeno

The canyons in the eastern foothills of the Colorado Rocky Mountains are home to an interesting ecological phenomenon. South-facing slopes in these canyons are covered with ponderosa pine, yucca, prickly pear cactus, and various grass species that thrive in warm, sunny, dry environments. In contrast, north-facing slopes are home to plants such as blue spruce, Douglas fir, and mountain maple that prefer cool, shady, moist conditions (Figure 3.1). Local differences in environmental conditions (**microclimate**), such as temperature and soil moisture, between the opposite slopes allow them to support species adapted to these different habitats. Not only do the species and microclimate differ, but ecological processes that occur in the two areas differ also.

The example above illustrates the different levels of ecological organization. All of the individuals of the same species (e.g., all of the ponderosa pine on the south-facing slope or all of the Douglas fir on the north-facing slope) living in the same area form a population. The populations of different species co-existing and interacting with one another on the north-facing or south-facing slopes form an ecological **community**. The interaction between the community and the abiotic aspects of the habitat (climate, soil, light) forms an ecosystem.

Temperature, water availability, nutrients, and light vary among habitats. The unique adaptations of a species allow individuals to function within a particular range of environmental conditions. Where conditions are optimal, individuals can survive and reproduce and populations can be maintained. If conditions are outside the optimal range, individuals may be able to grow but they may not have normal growth or be able to successfully reproduce. Under these conditions, populations can persist only if there are immigrants from other populations to replace those that die. Outside of the tolerable range of conditions, individuals cannot survive and populations cannot be maintained. For example, subalpine fir can grow in mountainous regions from approximately 10,000–12,000 feet. At the upper end

Figure 3.1 North-facing (A) and south-facing (B) slopes in a Rocky Mountain canyon. North-facing slopes favor plants that prefer cool, shady, moist conditions (blue spruce, Douglas fir, mountain maple). South-facing slopes favor plants that thrive in warm, sunny, dry environments (ponderosa pine, yucca, prickly pear cactus).

of these elevations, trees do not have their typical tall, straight growth, but rather grow as low, twisted shrubs (a growth form called **krumholtz** meaning "twisted wood"). Above this elevation (called the **treeline**), environmental conditions are too extreme for trees to grow at all.

The geographic area in which populations of a species occur is its **range**. Populations of a species are typically not found everywhere within its range, but rather occur in locations where appropriate habitat conditions are found. Species with wide habitat tolerances such as aspen and red maple have a larger range than species such as Georgia oak and seaside alder, which have narrower habitat tolerances and, therefore, a smaller geographic range.

SPECIES DIVERSITY

An important feature of the community is the **diversity** of species existing together. Species diversity of a community is determined by the number of different species (**richness**) and the relative numbers of individuals in each species (**evenness**). For example, consider two hypothetical plant communities each containing 100 individuals in five different species. In one community, there are 20 individuals of each species. In the other community there are 92 individuals of one species and two individuals of each of the remaining four species. Although their richness is identical, the first community is considered more diverse due to greater evenness among species. In general, plant communities near the tropics tend to have greater diversity due to higher richness and evenness of species than more temperate ecosystems, which often have lower richness and evenness.

In a community with low evenness, the one or few species that make up the majority of individuals are called the **dominant** species. For instance, oak-hickory forests of the Appalachian Mountains are dominated by various species of oaks and hickories, even though other tree species such as dogwood, maples, and sourwood are present. Tallgrass prairies are dominated by four grass species (big bluestem, switch grass, little bluestem, and Indian grass), but a variety of other plant species also grow there.

COMMUNITY STRUCTURE

A plant community is composed of species that occur together in a specific area. If the area being considered is relatively small, then a very specific community type can be identified. On a larger scale, the community descriptions tend to be broader. For example, when considering an area of several hundred hectares in the coastal plain of the Florida panhandle, one can identify a longleaf pine community. Over thousands of square miles, the longleaf pine community is one of several different community types that together comprise the southeastern evergreen–mixed hardwood forest community that extends across several states. Many other large-scale community types together make up the eastern deciduous forest community.

In most instances, communities do not have a definite boundary. Rather, they tend to transition from one community type into the next as environmental conditions such as temperature or water availability change. These transitional areas are called **ecotones** (Figure 3.2). If there is an abrupt change in abiotic conditions, such as soil type or between an agricultural area and an adjacent forest, the ecotone can be sharp and distinct. However, if conditions change gradually, the ecotone will be a more subtle transitional area.

Another significant feature of communities is their vertical structure (Figure 3.3). Plants grow to various heights, creating different vegetation layers within the community. The lowest growing plants form an herbaceous layer of small plants at ground level and a shrub layer composed of small woody, perennials. Trees compose all layers above the shrub layer. Smaller trees comprise the **understory** layer. Understory trees can be mature individuals of small species, such as dogwood and redbud, or young individuals of taller species. The tallest trees form the **canopy** layer. In tropical forests, an additional layer of **emergent** trees occurs. These are exceptionally tall trees whose crowns rise above the canopy layer.

The layers of vegetation play an important role in regulating light in the community. Communities such as grasslands have no canopy layer and, therefore, all of the photosynthesis takes place in the herbaceous and shrub layers. In forests, the crowns of canopy trees receive ample sunlight and are responsible for much of the photosynthesis in forests. If the canopy is continuous, lower layers will remain in shade and will not contain many plants, but if there are openings in the canopy, sunlight can penetrate to lower layers and support a greater diversity of plants below.

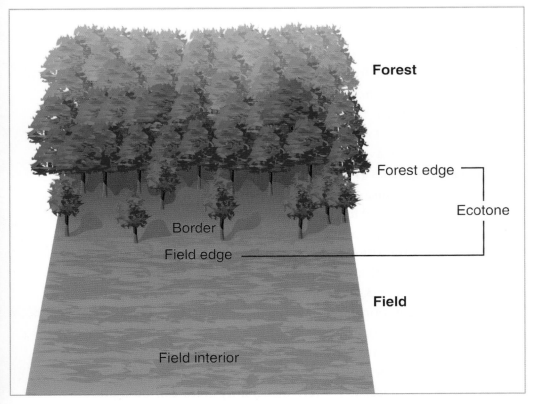

Figure 3.2 Most plant communities do not have definitive boundaries. Rather, they transition from one community type to the next (for example, from forest to field) as environmental conditions change. These transitional areas are called ecotones.

Vegetation layers also provide habitat for other species. Different bird species, for example, specialize their feeding and nesting in different vegetation layers. More layers mean more potential habitats for birds. Thus, plant communities with more vertical layers support a greater diversity of bird species than communities with fewer layers.

ECOSYSTEM FUNCTION

There are three essential components to a functioning ecosystem: a pool of nonliving nutrients and energy resources, **producers**

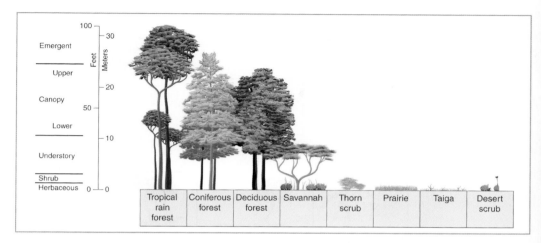

Figure 3.3 Plant communities have a vertical structure, creating different vegetation layers. The lowest growing plants are herbaceous species and shrubs at ground level. Smaller trees comprise the understory layer, while the tallest trees form a canopy layer. In tropical forests, there are also emergent trees whose crowns rise above even the canopy.

that draw from this nonliving pool of resources, and **consumers** (animals, bacteria, and fungi) that obtain their energy and nutrients from the producers (Figure 3.4).

Each organism fills a particular **niche** within a community. A species' niche reflects all of the ways it gathers and uses resources and interacts with other organisms within its habitat. The niche can essentially be thought of as the organism's job within the community. For example, plants fill the niche of producers within communities. Through photosynthesis, they provide the energy and nutrients that consumers depend on to survive.

As producers, plants form the base of the **food chain** and direct the flow of energy through the ecosystem. The process begins when carbon dioxide (CO_2) enters the leaf through openings called **stomata**. The photosynthetic enzyme in the **chloroplast** takes up the CO_2 inside the leaf (a process called **carbon fixation**) and begins the process of photosynthesis, in which the energy in light is used to assemble CO_2 into energy-rich sugars. These sugars

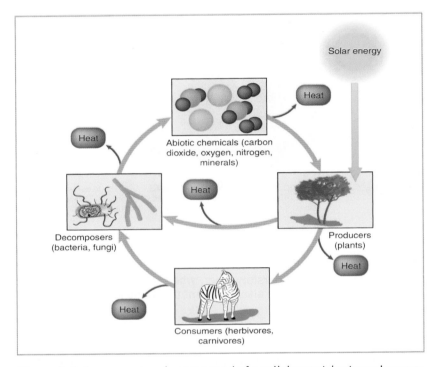

Figure 3.4 An ecosystem is composed of nonliving nutrients and energy resources, producers that draw from these resources, and consumers that get their energy from the producers. Decomposers then break down leaf litter and wastes into nutrients that can be cycled through the ecosystem again.

provide energy for metabolism in the plant and organic components needed to build the plant body. Oxygen (O_2) is released as a product of photosynthesis. The energy that is incorporated into the plant body is passed on to the consumers that eat the plant. Ultimately, the energy will be released back into the environment as heat and the nutrients will be returned to the soil.

Plants also direct the cycling of elements within ecosystems (see "Hubbard Brook Experiment" box). Many of the essential elements, such as nitrogen, phosphorus, calcium, and potassium, are stored in the soil in the form of organic matter from dead organisms and waste or inorganic minerals from rock. Nutrients in the soil are actively taken up by special proteins in the membranes of root cells that transport ions of specific nutrients into the root. The nutrients are then transported throughout the plant by water in the xylem. Inside the plant, they provide the building blocks for DNA, proteins, and other components of the living organism. Organic molecules produced in the plant will be consumed by herbivores that eat the plant. Then they will be passed along to other animals in the food chain that eat the herbivore. The ingested materials will eventually be returned to the soil in the form of wastes from plants and animals or when the animal dies. Leaves and branches that drop from the plant onto the ground form **leaf litter**. The leaf litter, animal wastes, and dead animals are eventually broken down by **decomposers**. These nutrients can then be taken up by a plant to cycle through the environment again.

Hubbard Brook Experiment

One of the most extensive studies of how vegetation affects nutrient cycling in ecosystems was conducted at the Hubbard Brook Experimental Forest in New Hampshire. Researchers first measured stream nutrient levels in the watershed of separate valleys. Nutrient levels were low in the streams and indicated little loss of nutrients through leaching from the soil. Next they cut all of the trees and killed all vegetation in one valley and left the others undisturbed as a control. The levels of water and nutrients in the streams of the manipulated and control valleys were then measured and compared. Nutrient levels continued to be low in the control streams. In the deforested watersheds, however, there was an increase in water run-off in the watershed and dramatic increases in stream nitrate and calcium levels. These results demonstrate that vegetation regulates nutrient availability and water dynamics of ecosystems. Intact vegetation and litter in the understory help store nutrients and keep them available for uptake by organisms in an ecosystem. Without vegetation, many nutrients are lost from the ecosystem through leaching and soil fertility rapidly declines.

PHOTOSYNTHESIS

Most plants use a photosynthetic pathway called C_3 **photosynthesis** (or the Calvin cycle) that works well in many environments (Figure 3.5). In hot, dry, sunny environments, however, C_3 photosynthesis does not always work efficiently. Under these conditions, plants close their stomata, which prevents CO_2 from entering the leaf and O_2 from leaving the leaf. The higher O_2 levels in the leaf cause the photosynthetic enzyme to begin fixing O_2. Instead of taking up CO_2 and producing sugars, this process of **photorespiration** consumes sugars that the plant has previously produced and releases CO_2

To cope with this problem, some plant species in arid, high light environments use a modified photosynthetic system known as C_4 **photosynthesis.** C_4 plants such as amaranth, pineapple, and many grasses have a modified internal leaf anatomy and specialized photosynthetic enzymes to minimize the occurrence of photorespiration. These modifications also allow C_4 plants to tolerate lower water availability than C_3 plants.

Cacti and other **succulent** plants in extremely hot, dry environments use a photosynthetic pathway called **Crassulacean Acid Metabolism (CAM) photosynthesis.** These plants open their stomata at night to release oxygen and take up carbon dioxide. The carbon dioxide is stored as malic acid within the plant cells. The plants close their stomata during the daytime and slowly release the carbon dioxide from the acid to use in photosynthesis. By opening their stomata only at night, they minimize water loss.

PRODUCTIVITY

The energy converted from sunlight into sugars by photosynthesis is called **primary productivity. Gross primary productivity (GPP)** is the total amount of energy converted by plants. The **net primary productivity (NPP)** is the amount of energy that remains after plants have met their own energetic needs through **respiration (R).** These energy relationships can be expressed by the mathematical

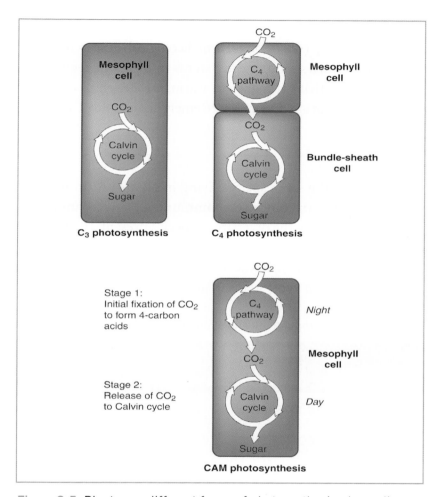

Figure 3.5 Plants use different forms of photosynthesis, depending on environmental conditions. Most plants use C_3 photosynthesis, which produces a 3-carbon sugar. Plants in hot, dry, sunny environments use C_4 photosynthesis. In extremely hot, dry environments, plants such as cacti use CAM photosynthesis, with CO_2 uptake taking place at night to minimize water loss.

formula: NPP = GPP–R. NPP is stored in the plant body as sugars, starch, and the plant body itself. It is the NPP that is available for consumers to eat and pass energy through the food chain. Productivity is typically expressed in terms of the mass of living organisms or **biomass** accumulated in an area over time (g/m^2/year) (see "Long-Term Ecological Research" box). Productivity varies among ecosystems in different regions. In general, productivity is higher in warm, wet tropical areas and lower in areas that are dry or are extremely hot or cold (Table 3.1).

Summary

Individuals of the same species living in an area form populations, which in turn comprise a community. Plant communities are characterized by the diversity of species present, their spatial structure, and the numbers of different vegetation layers. The community interacts with the abiotic environment as part of an ecosystem. Within ecosystems, plants direct the flow of energy

Table 3.1 Net Primary Productivity and Biomass of Different Habitats

Habitat (Biome)	NPP Range (g/m^2)	Average NPP (g/m^2)	Biomass per area (kg/m^2)	Average Biomass (kg/m^2)
Tropical Forest	1000–3500	2200	6–80	45
Temperate Deciduous Forest	600–2500	1200	6–60	30
Taiga	400–2000	800	6–40	20
Chaparral	250–1200	700	2–20	6
Savannah	200–2000	900	0.2–15	4
Prairie	200–1500	600	0.2–5	1.6
Tundra	10–400	140	0.1–3	0.6
Desert	10–250	90	0.1–4	0.7

Data from E.P. Odum and G.W. Barrett, *Fundamentals of Ecology*, 5th ed. Belmont, CA: Thompson Brooks/Cole, 2005, p. 89.

and the cycling of nutrients within a food chain. Ecosystems are often characterized by the amounts of energy converted through photosynthesis. A variety of photosynthetic pathways have evolved that allow plants to conduct photosynthesis effectively in their environment.

Long-Term Ecological Research

Because of the multitude of processes and interactions among the biotic and abiotic components of ecosystems, investigations of ecosystem dynamics require research programs that extend beyond the scope of a single researcher and involve collaborative efforts among many scientists. Likewise, comparisons among ecosystems in different areas are necessary to understand both the common processes of all ecosystems and the unique properties of each one. To promote large-scale, collaborative ecological studies, the Long-Term Ecological Research (LTER) program was established in 1977. The thrust of the program is to promote investigation of ecosystems over large areas and for long periods of time.

Initially, six locations were chosen for LTER sites, but the program now includes 26 sites that represent a diversity of ecosystems—tropical forests in Puerto Rico, The McMurdo Dry Valleys of Antarctica, tallgrass prairies in Kansas, and the urban environment of Baltimore, Maryland. Research at LTER sites focuses on five core areas: primary productivity, spatial and temporal dynamics of populations and communities, accumulation and decomposition of organic matter, nutrient cycling, and disturbance. These studies provide not only insights into basic ecological processes, but also essential data that can help find solutions to current ecological problems. For example, collection of climatic data among LTER sites provides evidence about the impacts of global climate change on dissimilar and widely separated ecosystems. Through coordination of research efforts, collaboration among researchers, and communication of findings, the LTER program provides a legacy of ecological research that benefits current and future generations.

4 Interactions Among Plants

When we try to pick out anything by itself,
we find it hitched to everything else in the universe.

— John Muir (1838–1914)
First president of the Sierra Club

Interactions Among Plants

A walnut tree might appear to be a passive component of its forest environment, living a solitary life, but this is not the case. It will interact with many other entities over the course of its lifetime. For example, it takes up water and nutrients from the soil that other nearby plants of the same or different species are also trying to acquire. Above ground, it must secure space in which to grow and absorb sunlight. Toward this end, its fruits release toxins into the ground as they decay, killing the seedlings of other plants that might try to germinate in the same place. Insects and other animals feed on the tree's leaves. Fungi and bacteria use the tree as a host. Squirrels eat some of its seeds, but disperse others to locations where the tree's offspring may germinate and grow.

Organisms living in the same location interact in many ways that can shape their growth and survival. Plants interact with other plants, as well as various animals, fungi, and bacteria. Plant ecologists classify these interactions based upon whether they benefit or inhibit the growth of one or both species. **Competition** has negative effects that harm both species when they exist together. **Parasitism** has a negative effect on one organism and a positive effect on the other when they interact, but the opposite effect on the two organisms when they do not come into contact with one another.

COMPETITION

Competition is the most common interaction between plants. Organisms must compete for limited resources (water, light, space, nutrients). Competition between members of the same species can be more intense than competition between different species because they fill an identical niche. Competition will result in co-existence (if the competitors are able to obtain sufficient resources) or exclusion (if one competitor can prevent the other from obtaining these resources). Competition also results in smaller plants that produce fewer flowers and seeds.

Self-thinning is another outcome of plant competition. Within a population, plant density may be very high when seeds first germinate. Some plants will acquire resources better and grow faster than others. Those plants that cannot acquire sufficient resources die. Thus, as the population density decreases (self-thins), survivors are able to grow to a larger size because competition for resources is reduced. For example, following forest fires, lodgepole pines release thousands of seeds to colonize the burned area. After several years, the population of young saplings is very thick. Unable to thrive in the shade of their faster-growing rivals, slower-growing trees will die, leaving a population in which individuals are evenly spaced and can obtain sufficient light.

COMMENSALISM AND PARASITISM

Epiphytes such as orchids, bromeliads, and ferns as well as different vines and lianas that grow on the branches and trunks of trees are examples of commensalism (Figure 4.1), a type of interaction in which one organism benefits and the other is not affected. These plants use the host tree as a location to grow. They attach to the bark with specialized roots that gather soil and leaves at their base. They absorb rainwater that flows along the trunk or, in the case of bromeliads, collect it in cup-shaped leaves. These plants typically do not harm the host unless their weight causes branches or the trunk to break.

Parasitism is an interaction in which an organism extracts energy and nutrients from its host. It is possible that parasites evolved from a species that originally had a commensal relationship with the host. Plants have evolved a variety of strategies to parasitize other plants. Seeds of species such as dodder, Indian pipe, and dwarf mistletoe germinate on or near their host and then grow specialized roots or stems that penetrate the host body to draw water, nutrients, and carbohydrates from its vascular tissue (Figure 4.2). These non-photosynthetic parasites are easily

Figure 4.1 Epiphytes are non-parasitic plants that grow on the branches and trunks of trees. Examples are orchids, bromeliads, ferns, and vines. They represent commensalism, an interaction in which one organism benefits without harming the other.

identified because they do not produce chlorophyll and therefore are not green. The common mistletoe is a **hemiparasite** because although it takes water from the host, it is capable of obtaining energy through its own photosynthesis.

Strangler figs are an example of the fine line between commensalism and parasitism. Strangler fig seeds germinate in the upper branches of tall tropical trees and for the first part of their life exist as epiphytes. They grow numerous roots to the

Figure 4.2 Dwarf mistletoe (A) parasitizes its host for water and nutrients. Common mistletoe (B) is a hemiparasite because it takes water from the host but produces its own energy through photosynthesis.

ground that eventually encircle and thicken around the host's trunk. In the canopy, the strangler fig leaves shade the host's leaves and, eventually, the host tree is starved for light and dies. Over time, the dead host decomposes, leaving the hollow latticework of the strangler fig trunk as a freestanding tree.

Although they do not draw water or nutrients from their host, they use its body for support until they can establish and out compete the host for light.

MUTUALISMS

In some instances, there is an interaction between individuals that is beneficial to both. These interactions are called **mutualisms.** For a mutualism to evolve and persist, each species must provide a benefit or service to the other that helps them survive better than when they occur alone.

One important mutualism for many species involves a symbiotic relationship between plants and **mycorrhizae** (fungi that associate with the plant's roots). Mycorrhizal fungi penetrate the root and grow into or between root cells or around the outer surface of the plant root. Filaments of the fungal body extend into the soil where they take up nutrients such as phosphate and transfer them to the plant. In exchange for the nutrients, mycorrhizae receive carbohydrates that serve as an energy source to promote their growth. Many trees depend on mycorrhize to establish seedlings. Orchid seeds are so small that seedlings are completely dependent on mycorrhize to provide nutrients to the young plant.

Another mutualism related to plant nutrition involves nitrogen-fixing bacteria. Plants in the bean family, legumes, frequently have mutualistic relationships with these bacteria. The bacteria infect the roots and form nodules on the roots. Inside the nodules, the bacteria convert nitrogen from the air into a form that plants can use. The plant provides the bacteria with carbohydrates and a place to live in return for this service.

Some plants form mutualisms with animals that protect them. Several ant species make their homes in the large thorns of acacia trees (Figure 4.3). A pregnant queen ant locates an unoccupied acacia, hollows out a thorn, and lays eggs. When larvae from the eggs mature, they become workers that excavate

Figure 4.3 Mutualisms are interactions between individuals that benefit both. Here, an acacia tree provides shelter and food to ants, who in turn attack intruders and kill seedlings that threaten "their" acacia.

other thorns and hollow out branches to form the nest for the colony. If animals attempt to feed on the plant, the ants swarm out of the nest to attack the intruder. Likewise, ants patrol the area around their tree to kill seedlings that sprout in the immediate vicinity or cut back branches of neighboring plants that come in contact with "their" acacia.

In exchange for protection, the acacia provides not just a home but also nutritious nectar for the adult ants to feed upon.

Some acacias also produce protein-rich structures called **Beltian bodies** on the tips of leaves that the ants clip off and feed to their developing larvae.

HERBIVORY

While some plant-animal interactions benefit the plant, others do not. **Herbivory** is one of the most common interactions between plants and animals (see "Carnivorous Plants" box, Figure 4.4). **Herbivores** are animals that eat plants. **Grazers** such as bison, antelope, and even grasshoppers eat mainly grasses. **Browsers** such as deer, squirrels, and giraffes eat leaves and other tissues from woody plants. **Granivores** such as mice and ants and **frugivores** such as monkeys, bats, and some reptiles eat seeds and fruits, respectively. The fundamental impact of herbivory on a plant is

Carnivorous Plants

Venus flytraps, pitcher plants, and sundews are plants that turn the tables on the animal kingdom. All of these species produce structures that trap and digest insects. The leaves of the Venus flytrap have small hairs on their inner surface. When an insect brushes against these hairs, the leaves shut, trapping the insect inside. The pitcher plant lures its victims by producing nectar around the rim of its pitcher-shaped leaves. Insects and even small mammals that sample the nectar slip and fall into the fluid at the base of the hollow leaf. Unable to climb out due to the downward growing hairs that line the inner surface of the leaf, the animals drown and are slowly digested. Sundews capture their next meal's attention by coating hairs on the upper surfaces of their leaves with digestive juices that glisten like nectar. An insect struggling to free itself from the sticky hairs is slowly enveloped by the leaf and digested. Carnivorous plants gain nutrients (primarily nitrogen) rather than energy from their prey, which they need to help them survive in the nutrient-poor soils where they typically grow.

Figure 4.4 Carnivorous plants such as the Venus flytrap (shown above) turn the tables on the animal kingdom, trapping and consuming small insects as a source of nutrients.

the loss of energy that the plant has fixed and accumulated through photosynthesis. Annually, herbivores consume approximately 10% of terrestrial net primary productivity.

Plants have evolved various defenses to repel and protect against herbivores. One basic defense is the composition of the plant body itself. Plant tissues have a high content of complex carbohydrates such as cellulose and lignin that make up the plant cell wall. These complex carbohydrates are difficult to digest and only those animals with specialized digestive systems can eat them.

Plants also use structural modifications to deter herbivores. Spines and thorns on leaves, branches, and twigs may prevent herbivores from biting into a plant. In some cases, the thorns come off of the plant and imbed in the herbivore's mouth. Other species retain the thorn on the plant to repel the next animal that attempts to feed. Stinging nettles utilize an even more diabolical form of protection. These plants produce millions of hollow hairs on the surface of their leaves and stems. Each hair contains a toxic chemical that is produced by a gland at its base. When an animal attempts to eat the nettle, the tip of the hair breaks off and the hair inserts itself into the animal. The gland then contracts, injecting the toxin into the animal. The intense burning sensation caused by the toxin immediately signals to the herbivore that this plant offers only pain for the palate.

Some plants use **mimicry** to deceive herbivores. Dead nettles have leaves and a growth form that mimics stinging nettles. Herbivores who have encountered a stinging nettle avoid dead nettles even though they do not produce any toxic chemicals. Certain species of passionflower produce small bulbous structures on their leaves and stems that resemble the egg sacs of insects whose larvae eat the plant's leaves. Insects avoid laying their eggs on plants where another female has already laid her eggs. Thus, the plant is able to fool these parasites, causing them to seek out some other, less well defended host.

Chemical defenses that cause illness and even death to the unwary herbivore are quite common in plants (Table 4.1). **Alkaloids** such as caffeine, mescaline, and nicotine may disrupt an herbivore's metabolic processes or cause its nervous system to malfunction. These poisons are produced at little energetic cost to the plant and are easily transported around the plant to sites where they are needed. Some plants produce cyanide-containing compounds in their seeds, leaves, and roots, which block the action of enzymes necessary for energy transfer within an herbivore's cells (see "Allelopathy" box). Plants such as soybean and birch produce

Table 4.1 Defensive Chemicals Used by Plants

CHEMICAL COMPOUND	SOURCE	EFFECT
COMPLEX CARBOHYDRATES:		
Cellulose	All plants	Reduces Digestibility
Hemicellulose	All plants	Reduces Digestibility
ALKALOIDS:		
Atropine	Datura	Affects nervous system
Caffeine	Coffee	Stimulant
Conine	Poison hemlock	Neurotoxin
Mescaline	Peyote cactus	Affects nervous system
Morphine	Opium poppy	Affects nervous system
Nicotine	Tobacco	Affects nervous system
Tomatine	Tomato	Disrupts membranes
TERPENOIDS:		
Digitalin	Foxglove	Cardiac stimulant
Oleandrin	Oleander	Cardiac toxin
Tetrahydrocannabinol	Cannabis	Affects nervous system
PHENOLICS:		
Lignin	Woody tissues	Binds proteins, reduces digestibility

chemicals that are hormone mimics that disrupt development of larvae that ingest them. Other compounds such as tannins and phenolics act by either reducing the palatability of a plant or by binding with digestion proteins to make the herbivore sick.

Herbivores, in return, can evolve tolerance to some toxic chemicals. The caterpillars of certain butterfly species, such as the monarch, have evolved the ability to tolerate the highly toxic compounds found in the milkweeds on which they feed. This allows them to take advantage of a food source that is not available to other herbivores. But the relationship between the milkweed and its predators does not end there. Not only do the caterpillars tolerate the toxin, they also incorporate it into their own bodies, defending themselves against predators such as birds. This relationship is a perfect example of **coevolution**, in which evolutionary changes in one species drive corresponding evolutionary changes in another.

Coevolutionary changes and adaptations can have a cascade of ecological and evolutionary consequences. For example, even though the viceroy butterfly does not feed on milkweeds and is not toxic, potential predators avoid eating it because its appearance

Allelopathy

While many plants use chemicals to defend against attacks by herbivores, species such as eucalyptus, sagebrush, chamise, and rhododendron produce chemicals that have a negative effect on other plants. Allelopathy is a strategy in which plants produce volatile chemicals in their leaves. When the leaves drop to the ground, the chemicals are released into the soil where they accumulate and prevent seed germination. The allelopathic chemicals maintain a bare zone that prevents other plants from colonizing the area and competing for resources. Allelopathy is particularly common in desert scrub and chaparral ecosystems where resources are sparse.

mimics that of the monarch. These relationships among species serve as excellent examples of what has been called Commoner's First Rule of Ecology: everything is connected to everything else.

Summary

Plants interact with many other organisms within their environment. Most of the interactions between plants are competition, although some plants can be parasitic on other plants. Plants have beneficial interactions with some organisms such as mutualisms between plants and mycorrhizal fungi and nitrogen-fixing bacterial. Other interactions such as herbivory can have a detrimental impact on the plant. A wide variety of structural and chemical defenses have evolved that help plants defend against herbivores as well as other plants.

To people who grumbled at the weather he recommended a garden,
"as the best of remedies for that commonest of melancholies,"
for there is no weather that did not suit some plant. In the hottest
and driest time the portulacas are burning red in the sand.
In cool and cloudy weather the soft morning-glories remain open until noon.
When the soil is soaked with rain the irises are in their glory.

— Liberty Hyde Bailey

Plant Biogeography

Modern plant ecology owes much to early studies of plant biogeography. Pioneering botanists in the 18th and 19th centuries such as Carl Wildenow (1765–1812) and Alexander von Humbolt (1769–1859) compared vegetation patterns among different regions of the Earth. Plant ecologists of the time knew that, on a local scale, different environmental conditions supported different vegetation. For example, plants that grow along rivers differ from plants that grow along dry mountain ridges. Plant biogeographers showed that the same principle applies on a global scale. Warm, rainy equatorial regions support forests of gigantic trees and tremendous species diversity. Drier, central regions of continents are typically dominated by grasslands. Cool areas at the tops of high mountains support plant communities similar to those found in polar regions. These observations led to the development of the general principle that, on a global scale, areas with similar climate support similar types of vegetation, whether across a large area of one continent or on separate continents.

Biomes are large geographic regions of terrestrial habitat that support similar types of communities and ecosystems (Figure 5.1). Biomes are typically characterized by and differentiated from one another by their vegetation. Plants within a a particular habitat are adapted to specific climatic conditions. Thus, the same biome on different continents tends to have the same appearance and structure because plants must utilize similar traits and strategies to survive in that environment. For example, desert plants must be able to tolerate extreme heat and drought. Thus, deserts in North America and Africa are home to plants with succulent, water-storing stems, highly reduced leaves, and thorny defense mechanisms.

THE DISTRIBUTION OF BIOMES

A variety of environmental factors shape the distribution of biomes, particularly temperature and moisture (Figure 5.2).

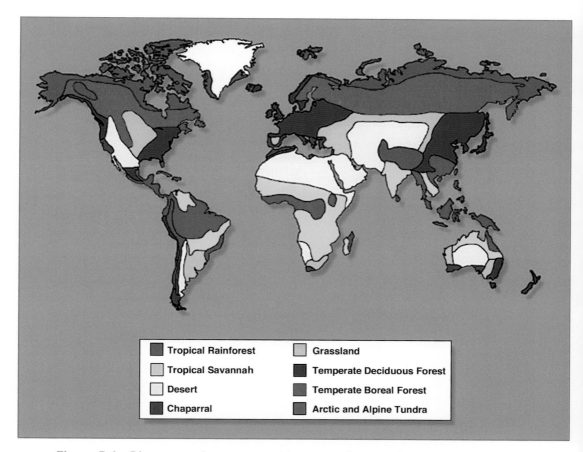

Figure 5.1 Biomes are large geographic areas of terrestrial habitat with similar ecosystems. Terrestrial biomes of the world are illustrated in the map above.

Temperature and moisture are important because they encompass the effects of many other factors, such as latitude, ocean currents, and prevailing winds that shape regional climate. Although they can be considered individually, temperature and moisture also interact to shape biome characteristics and distributions.

Although temperature and moisture are the main factors, other environmental variables influence habitat distribution as well. Variation in topography, irregular shapes and locations of continents, temperatures of nearby ocean currents, characteristics of

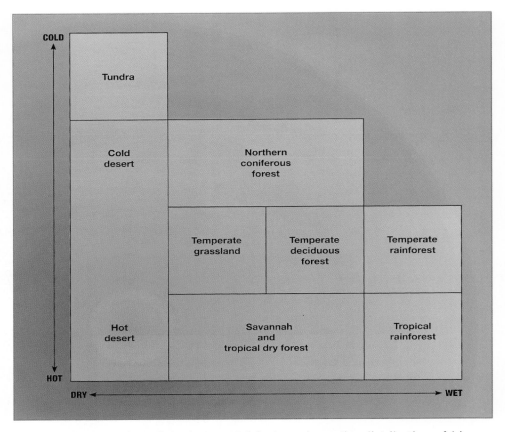

Figure 5.2 A number of environmental factors shape the distribution of biomes around the world, especially temperature and moisture. Temperature and moisture also interact to shape biome characteristics.

prevailing winds, and the amount of a hemisphere covered by land or water cause regional climatic variation which further shapes biome distribution. Thus, rather than occurring as distinct bands corresponding to latitude, biomes are distributed in more of a mosaic pattern around the planet.

MAJOR TERRESTRIAL BIOMES

Plant ecologists have developed different biome classification systems, but most categorize biomes as forests, grasslands, or deserts.

Within these broad groupings, biomes are further characterized based upon the general pattern of temperatures. Eight of the most common biomes are described below (see "Biomes of the Past" box).

Forests

Areas with the highest rainfall generally support the growth of trees. Trees are large organisms and require large amounts of water to survive. However, as average temperature decreases, the amount of water required to support a forest decreases. Three main types of forest are tropical forests, temperate forests, and taiga (Figure 5.3).

Biomes of the Past

The current types and distribution of biomes on Earth has not always been as it is now. Evolution of new life forms, shifts in climatic conditions, and never-ending geologic processes have caused many changes in the distribution and composition of biomes. During the Carboniferous Period (300 million years ago), Earth's climate was much warmer and the landscape was covered with extensive swamp forests. These forests were dominated by gigantic ancestors of present-day horsetails, club mosses, and ferns. In the Oligocene Epoch (33 million years ago), the central regions of continents became much drier. Grasses, which were able to tolerate the dry conditions in these regions, evolved during this time and gave birth to extensive prairies. In response, grazing species of animals such as horses evolved and thrived. During the ice ages that occurred over 50,000 years ago, extensive coniferous forests were found much further south than they are today. As the planet warmed and glaciers retreated, plants of tropical biomes expanded their ranges to the north and south while cold-adapted plants retreated poleward. These past events serve as clear evidence that when climate change occurs, species, communities, and ecosystems will respond ecologically and evolutionarily.

Figure 5.3 Temperate deciduous forest biomes occur in mid-latitude regions of North America, Europe, and Asia. Many trees in these forests drop their leaves and go dormant in the winter.

Tropical Forests

Tropical forests are found in equatorial regions of South America, Southeast Asia, and Africa. These areas have little variation in day length or temperature. Tropical forests typically receive 200–400 cm (78–156 inches) of precipitation per year, although some can receive in excess of 500 cm (195 inches) annually. **Tropical rain forests** receive precipitation throughout the year, but **tropical dry forests** experience a period of drought followed by a monsoon season in which there is abundant rainfall.

There is little leaf litter on the tropical forest floor because warm temperatures and high water availability promote rapid decomposition of leaves and other organic material. Nutrients are taken up quickly by plants or are lost by leaching in water, which causes tropical soils to be low in nutrient content.

The dominant plants of tropical forests are enormous trees. The crowns of the large trees form a continuous canopy overhead that prevents light from penetrating to the forest floor. Thus, herbaceous plants are scattered and often restricted to locations on the forest floor under openings in the canopy. Some of the tallest trees extend beyond the continuous canopy and are called emergents. Below the canopy there can be several understory layers of trees and shrubs, which are adapted to live in the deep shade of the canopy. The multiple layers of vegetation between the forest floor and the top of the canopy provide habitats for plants such as epiphytes, lianas, and other organisms to use.

Tropical rain forests make up the most diverse biome on Earth. Although they cover only 7% of the Earth's surface, they are home to over 50% of the known species of organisms in addition to many more, as yet undiscovered, species. Species diversity in tropical forests can be four to five times greater than that of temperate forests. Within a single hectare (about 2.5 acres) of tropical forest, it is not uncommon to find over 200 different tree species.

Temperate Forests

Temperate forests occur in mid-latitude regions of North America, Europe, and Asia. They receive 75–300 cm (29–117 inches) of precipitation, which is often distributed evenly throughout the year. Because they are outside the tropics, these regions have cooler average temperatures and noticeable seasonal changes. The growing season in these areas can be four to eight months in length. In **temperate deciduous forests,** many species, particularly trees, have evolved the strategy of dropping their leaves and going dormant during the unfavorable growing conditions of winter. Where winters are more severe or there is a pronounced summer drought, **temperate coniferous forests** are found.

Compared to tropical forests, temperate forests have lower species diversity. One typically finds only 20–30 different tree species per hectare. Temperate forests have a canopy, but it is neither as continuous nor are there as many canopy layers as in tropical forests. Because the canopy is more open, sunlight can penetrate to the forest floor, supporting a diverse understory layer of herbs and shrubs. These forests also have a well developed layer of leaf litter on the forest floor, which indicates that nutrients cycle more slowly through this system.

Taiga

The taiga (also known as temperate evergreen or montane coniferous forest) is the coldest of all forest types. This biome occurs between 50° and 65° north latitude as well as at high elevations in mountainous regions at lower latitudes. In the taiga, temperatures can range from –30°C to over 25°C during the course of a year. Annual precipitation ranges between 30 cm and 60 cm (12–24 inches), much of it in the form of snow. Summers tend to be fairly dry.

Taiga forests have low species diversity, often containing fewer than five different tree species per hectare. In extreme cases, extensive forests covering thousands of hectares may contain only one or two species. Coniferous evergreens such as pine, spruce, and fir dominate the taiga, though deciduous aspen, willow, and birch can be found in moist areas. High tree density can cause dark conditions in the understory of some forests. However, in some montane coniferous forests, regular fires during the dry summer months decrease tree density and allow light to reach the forest floor, supporting the growth of perennial grasses, herbs, and shrubs.

Grasslands

In areas where precipitation is too low to support the growth of trees for a given temperature range, grasses dominate the landscape.

Grasslands occur on every continent, often in the interior regions. Fire, large herbivore populations, and regular droughts are some of the main factors that promote the occurrence of grasslands. As with forests, grasslands can be differentiated depending on the temperature and seasonality of a region (Figure 5.4).

Savanna

Savannas are found in tropical and subtropical areas of Australia, central and southern Africa, and central and southern South America. They often occur in transitional areas between rain forests and deserts. There is strong seasonality in the savanna, typically an extended period of drought and warm temperatures lasting seven to ten months. Much of the annual rainfall is restricted to the short rainy season that follows the drought.

Savannas are open grasslands with widely scattered trees, many of which are legumes that function in soil nitrogen fixation. Fires, frequently started by lightning during the rainy season, prevent young trees from becoming established, thereby keeping tree density low. Although plant diversity is low in these extensive grasslands, they support a diversity of grazing mammals that migrate in response to patterns of rainfall and drought.

Temperate Grasslands/Prairies

Temperate grasslands, or **prairies**, grow across interior regions of North America and Eurasia, and in the southeastern coastal area of South America. Temperatures fluctuate from below 0°C in the winter to almost 30°C in the summer. Much of the precipitation comes during the summer growing season.

Prairies contain a diversity of grasses and herbs. As with the savanna, regular fires suppress the establishment of trees and maintain the dominance of grasses. Likewise, the dense network of grass roots immediately absorbs water and hinders the establishment of trees. Only along waterways can trees establish and persist. Prairies frequently have deep, nutrient-rich soils.

Figure 5.4 Where precipitation is too low to support trees, grasses dominate the landscape. Grasslands are on every continent and support populations of large grazing animals such as bison.

Decomposition is slow in these dry ecosystems, but fire accelerates the breakdown of organic material and nutrient cycling in the prairie. Prairies, like other grasslands, support populations of large grazing mammals (such as bison on the prairies of North America).

Tundra
The coldest grasslands are called tundra. This biome is restricted to polar regions (**arctic tundra**) and to mountaintops above

treeline (**alpine tundra**) (see "Elevation and Latitude" box, Figure 5.5). Average temperature is often at or below freezing and annual precipitation (mostly in the form of snow) is typically around 25 cm (10 inches). The growing season is very short, only 2–3 months in many regions. During summer, the snow melts, saturating the ground to form bogs and shallow ponds. The soil freezes during the long winter. Close below the surface of the nutrient-poor soil is a perpetually frozen layer of **permafrost**.

Plant diversity is low in the tundra. Vegetation is mostly limited to grasses, **sedges**, mosses, and lichens. To survive the harsh tundra climate, plants must adapt to the extremely short growing season. Many of the plants are herbaceous perennials that use nutrient reserves stored in underground structures such as corms, bulbs, and rhizomes to produce leaves quickly when conditions become favorable. Some species use a strategy called **preformation** in which flower buds are slowly produced several years in advance of their actual blooming so that reproduction can take place immediately in the extremely short growing season.

Elevation and Latitude

Elevation and latitude have similar impacts on climate and, consequently, biome distribution. Average temperature decreases from the equator to the poles and also as elevation increases. This change in temperature as latitude or elevation changes is the **lapse rate**. In general, there is a change in average temperature of 1°C per 100 miles traveled north or south and a change of 1°C per 100 meters elevation change. Plant ecologists have observed that changes in biome distribution with increased latitude are similar to changes in biome distribution with increased elevation. Thus, as one ascends a mountain, there are changes in biome distribution that correspond to changes observed as one travels to a higher latitude.

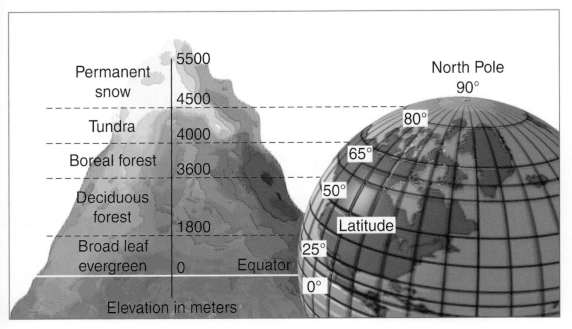

Figure 5.5 Elevation and latitude have similar impacts on climate and biome distribution. So, as one ascends a mountain, there are changes in biomes that correspond to changes seen as one travels to a higher latitude.

DESERT

Deserts are the driest biome of all. Precipitation can be as much as 50 cm (20 inches) per year, but it is often much lower. The driest deserts in Chile, Africa, and central Australia receive less than 2 cm (0.78 inches) per year. One of the main factors shaping the location of major deserts is their location near 30° north and south latitudes (Figure 5.6). These latitudes are subject to extremely dry prevailing winds that evaporate what little moisture there is from the soil.

All deserts are dry, but not all of them are hot. It is true that temperatures soar in the hot deserts of southwestern North America and north Africa. However, in cold deserts such as Asia's Gobi Desert, temperatures are above freezing during the short growing season, but plunge to well below freezing during the winter.

Open expanses of bare, exposed soil and rock are common in the desert. The few plants that live there are often succulent perennials that store water in their stems and leaves. Other perennial species are **drought deciduous**, which produce highly reduced leaves when moisture is available, but shed them as conditions become more arid. Annual species in the desert may remain dormant as seeds in the soil for many years until rain cues germination.

CHAPARRAL

One important biome that does not fit neatly into the categories of forest, grassland, or desert is the **chaparral** or Mediterranean scrub forest (Figure 5.7). This biome is typically located around the Mediterranean Sea, and coastal areas of southern California, Chile, southwest Africa, and southwest Australia. These temperate zone areas are adjacent to cool ocean currents that strongly influence the local climate. In the chaparral, winters are cool, wet, and mild, but summers are long, hot, and dry. The plants that dominate the chaparral are typically scrubby, thorny plants, such as scrub oaks and eucalyptus, that grow in dense thickets. They produce small, leathery, evergreen leaves that can tolerate the harsh summer conditions. Small annual plants also grow in the chaparral for brief periods immediately following winter rains.

Fire is very important in this biome. Seeds of chaparral species often require fire to stimulate seed germination. Aboveground structures of the shrubby plants may burn in a fire, but they quickly resprout from the roots after the fire. Not only do chaparral plants require fire, many can also promote it. The leaves of these species produce flammable chemicals which ignite easily and cause fires to be extremely hot. Because this biome is dry, the leaves dropped from plants accumulate and eventually burn. Nutrients tied up in these leaves are then released, making them available to other plants. These fires also reduce population density and make space available for other plants to grow.

Figure 5.6 Deserts are the driest biome of all. There are open expanses of exposed soil and rock and the few plants that live there are often succulent perennials that can store water.

Summary

Global climate patterns influence the distribution of vegetation on Earth. Biomes are large terrestrial regions that support similar vegetation. The main climatic factors that shape plant biogeography are temperature and moisture. Ecologists classify different biomes based upon the structure of the dominant vegetation. Forest biomes occur where there is sufficient moisture

Figure 5.7 The chaparral or Mediterranean scrub biome is dominated by scrubby, thorny plants that grow in dense thickets.

to support trees. Warm areas support tropical forests, while cooler areas support temperate forests and taiga. Where there is less precipitation, grassland biomes occur. In warmer areas the biome is a savannah, and in cooler areas the biome is a prairie or tundra. Deserts and chaparral are two other habitats that occur in drier locations.

6 The Changing Ecosystem

I think there will be radical changes. But I don't actually think that within the next 100 years the natural world will be reduced to rats and cockroaches, nor do I think that the plant world will be reduced to some kind of desert.

— David Attenborough

The Changing Ecosystem

In 2003, almost 5,000,000 acres burned in wildland fires throughout the United States.[1] Some of these fires did little damage to the vegetation, while others completely destroyed all plants in the community. The charred landscape following a severe fire can give the immediate impression that the burned area is lifeless and will remain so, but that is not the case. After even the most devastating fire, plants are able to colonize a site and reestablish a community. The process may be slow, but the plants do return (Figure 6.1).

Disturbance refers to any force or phenomenon in the environment that disrupts the standing vegetation. **Succession** is the series of predictable, cumulative changes in the composition and characteristics of a plant community that follows disturbance. The manner in which vegetation is disturbed and replaced involves biotic and abiotic interactions that shape the ecosystem.

CHARACTERISTICS OF DISTURBANCES

Each disturbance can be characterized by three features that describe its impact on an ecosystem: intensity, frequency, and scale. Intensity is the magnitude of the physical force, such as the strength of the wind or heat of the fire. Frequency is the time between disturbance events and scale is the spatial extent of a disturbance. All three are highly interrelated. In mountainous regions, for example, small rock slides may occur frequently over an entire mountainside but infrequently at a specific site. Severe avalanches that involve an entire mountainside, however, are extremely infrequent and are much more devastating to vegetation than lower intensity rock slides.

FIRE—A MAJOR ECOLOGICAL FORCE

Any physical force in the environment can cause a disturbance: wind, floods, earthquakes, and avalanches can damage vegetation; epidemic outbreaks of herbivorous insects can also devastate landscapes. However, of all forms of disturbance, none has

Figure 6.1 Globally, nothing has done more to shape the evolution of plant species and the dynamics of ecosystems as fire. Even after the most devastating fire, plants can reestablish a community.

done more to shape the evolution of species and the dynamics of ecosystems as fire. Globally, fire shapes large expanses of vegetation such as prairies, chaparral, savannas, and coniferous forests. It has a tremendous influence on the dynamics and characteristics of ecosystems in these biomes. Fire has also shaped the evolution of plant traits to not only protect against fires, but even to promote its occurrence.

Surface fires occur above ground, where they typically burn quickly and are not extremely hot. As the fire moves along the ground, it consumes leaf litter, shrubs, and other small plants. The bases of larger trees may be scorched, but are not usually severely damaged. Soil insulates and prevents surface fires from heating deeply and damaging roots, tubers, bulbs, or seeds that are underground.

Crown fires are the dramatic wildland fires most people envision (Figure 6.2). These fires spread from treetop to treetop. If there is a large amount of fuel on the ground, surface fires can burn hot enough to ignite branches and become crown fires. Crown fires burn extremely hot and can even generate their own powerful winds that carry flames through the forest rapidly.

The frequency and intensity of fires varies among ecosystems. Longleaf pine forests experience surface fires on 2–3 year cycles. Grasslands typically experience a fire every three years. In contrast, fires in Canadian spruce-hemlock-pine forests can be separated by over 200 years. Different types of fires have differing frequencies. Red pine forests experience light surface fires every 5–30 years and intense crown fires every 100–300 years. Fire scale also varies among ecosystems. Coniferous forests often have extensive fires over large areas, while fires in deciduous forests are typically restricted to warm dry slopes and ridges.

Fire requires a source of ignition, oxygen, and fuel to burn (Figure 6.3). Lightning strikes are the most common natural ignition source. Oxygen is readily available in the atmosphere,

Figure 6.2 In a crown fire, flames leap from treetop to treetop. Crown fires burn extremely hot and can even generate their own powerful winds.

and accumulated living and dead plant tissues provide fuel. Weather conditions strongly influence fuel flammability: for example, prairie fires typically occur during the drought conditions of late summer when leaf litter is extremely dry.

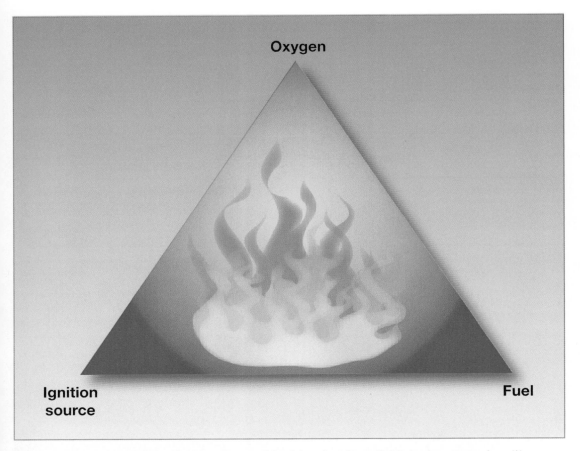

Figure 6.3 Fire requires a source of ignition (such as lightning), oxygen (readily available in the atmosphere), and fuel to burn (living and dead plant tissues).

The time interval between fires dictates fuel availability. Longer intervals between fires lead to greater fuel accumulation and, eventually, increased fire intensity. Ponderosa pine forests, for example, have an open, park-like appearance when regular surface fires are allowed to burn the area, removing fallen branches, leaf litter, and even pine seedlings. If fires are suppressed, tree density increases and plant litter accumulates on the ground, so that when there is a fire it will be more intense and far more damaging to the ecosystem.

Fire has many direct effects on the environment. For example, extremely hot fires destroy soil structure, which decreases soil permeability to water and can lead to severe erosion on the burned site. Although fire destroys standing vegetation and can even kill dormant seeds in the soil, fire also has beneficial effects. It removes dead wood and other plant material that can harbor pathogens. In grasslands and coniferous forests, decomposition is slow, leaving nutrients tied up in leaf litter. Fire rapidly breaks down and mineralizes these nutrients, making them available for plants. In grasslands, fire kills tree saplings and allows grasses to retain their dominance. Fire even prepares the seedbed for species such as pines whose seeds germinate rapidly in the warm, sunny conditions that follow a fire.

Plants use various strategies to cope with fire. Tree species such as pitch pine and chestnut oak produce thick bark that insulates the tree and protects it against surface fires. Trees with thinner bark such as dogwood and hickory are more susceptible to damage by surface fires. Grasses, aspen, and scrub oaks use a strategy of recovery after fire. Although the aboveground part of the plant is damaged, roots and trunks can sprout rapidly after fire to reestablish on the burned site. Other species are adapted to colonize burned sites—fire stimulates germination of mesquite and ceanothus seeds.

Serotiny is a strategy used by fire-dependent pines such as table mountain pine, lodgepole pine, and Bishop pine. Serotinous cones stay closed until heated by a fire (Figure 6.4) (see "Fire Ecology of Table Mountain Pine" box), then the cones slowly open after the fire passes to release their seeds onto the burned area. Finally, some plants have traits that actually promote fire. Many of the shrubs in the chaparral produce highly flammable compounds in their leaves that promote fires, thus clearing sites so their seeds have room to germinate and establish new plants. Fire-promoting species such as these sacrifice the individual plant to promote persistence of the species.

Figure 6.4 Serotinous cones, such as these from the table mountain pine, stay closed until heated by fire, then they slowly open and release their seeds after the fire passes.

SUCCESSION

Ecologists differentiate two types of succession. **Primary succession** is the series of changes in a plant community that occurs on bare substrates, such as exposed bedrock, or sand dunes that have not supported vegetation. **Secondary succession** is the series of changes that occurs in a plant community where the vegetation has been disturbed, but the soil remains.

The sequence of changes in a community undergoing succession is called a **sere**. The different recognizable communities that occur throughout a sere are called **seral stages.** The first is the pioneer stage in which species that can tolerate the extreme conditions of a recently disturbed or newly exposed site colonize and establish. Next come intermediate seral stages in which

Fire Ecology of Table Mountain Pine

Table mountain pine, a species found only in the southern Appalachian Mountains, is completely dependent on fire. It produces highly serotinous cones and requires the environmental conditions that follow severe fires in order to establish new trees.

The changing history of fire in the southern Appalachian Mountains continues to shape the distribution and occurrence of this species. Prior to the arrival of humans, table mountain pine was restricted to dry ridges and mountaintops where lightning-initiated fires occurred with sufficient frequency to maintain this species. Later, Native Americans used fire to hunt and clear land for agriculture. Lowland fires would have spread onto mountain slopes, creating more habitat for table mountain pines to colonize. European and American settlers continued this practice of using fire to clear lands on an even greater scale, which allowed table mountain pine to expand its range.

Although human activities in the past allowed table mountain pine to invade previously uninhabitable localities, current forest management practices are having the opposite effect. Policies to suppress all wildland fires in this region are allowing succession to proceed and stands of table mountain pine are being replaced by other species. Even ridgetop populations of table mountain pine are being lost. Experiments in which large tracts of land are burned are showing that table mountain pine is not regenerating as expected. This indicates that factors beyond burning alone are shaping table mountain pine regeneration and further research is needed. This, coupled with ecologically sound fire policies, may enable scientists to develop effective strategies to protect this tree species.

pioneer species become less common and later successional species begin to populate and dominate the site. If uninterrupted, succession will proceed to the final seral stage, the **climax community**. The composition of the climax community is determined by a site's specific microclimate and soil conditions. This community is self-sustaining and will not undergo further significant changes in species composition or structure unless disturbed. For example, in the Appalachian Mountains, the climax community in a moist valley contains a mixture of oak, magnolia, and hickory, while dry ridges are dominated by pines. Without disturbance, these communities will persist in a stable equilibrium.

Primary Succession

Primary succession is extremely slow because soil must be developed on a bare substrate (Figure 6.5). The process begins when lichens colonize bare rock. Mild acids released by the lichens and repeated freezing and thawing of water that seeps into cracks act to fracture and break the rock into small pieces, which provide the mineral component for soil formation. Dead tissues from the lichens and materials blown by the winds accumulate and mix with the rock particles to add organic material to the forming soil. This initial seral stage can take hundreds of years (see "Primary Succession on Granite Outcrops" box).

Eventually, mosses and other small plants begin to grow in the thin soils of these sites. Greater leaf production by these plants adds more organic material to the soil. Carbonic acid (formed when CO_2 released from roots combines with soil water) breaks down the rocks and accelerates the pace of soil formation. Larger plants such as grasses, perennial herbs, and shrubs next colonize the site. Finally, if climatic conditions are favorable, trees will eventually grow where there was once only bare rock.

Estimates of how long the process of primary succession will take have been made for some plant communities. It has been

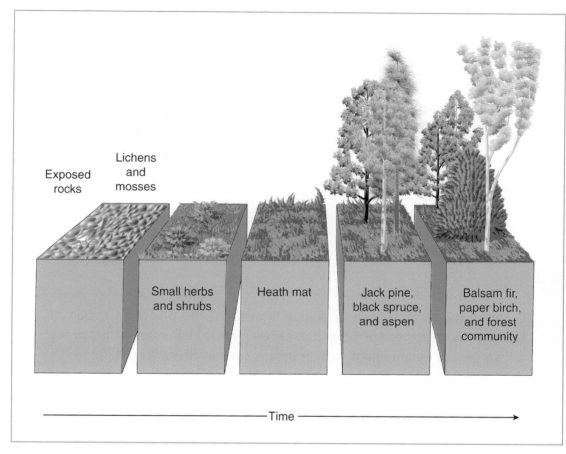

Exposed rocks

Lichens and mosses

Small herbs and shrubs

Heath mat

Jack pine, black spruce, and aspen

Balsam fir, paper birch, and forest community

Time

Figure 6.5 In primary succession, a series of changes occur to establish a plant community on bare substrates, such as exposed rocks, that have not supported vegetation before. It is a slow process that occurs over many years.

estimated that it will take 400 years for a tropical forest to develop on a lava flow in tropical Pacific islands. In the Hoh Valley in Washington, it can take 700 years for a spruce-hemlock forest to develop on a bare river terrace. Over 1,000 years are needed for a deciduous forest to develop on sand dunes surrounding Lake Michigan. And finally, it can take over 5,000 years for a moss-birch-tussock grass community to develop on glacier debris in Alaska. These estimates show that speed of succession is related to climate. Where temperatures are warmer and there is greater water availability, succession proceeds more rapidly.

Secondary Succession

Secondary succession moves faster than primary succession (Figure 6.6). This is largely due to the fact that soil is already present. The presence of plants and dormant seeds that survived the disturbance promotes more rapid establishment of plants in the disturbed site. However, it is important to remember that a severe disturbance, such as an intense fire that devastates the vegetation and soil, will slow the rate of

Primary Succession on Granite Outcrops

Granite rock outcrops can be found throughout the piedmont region of Georgia. The outcrops are either flat, exposed areas of granite just below the soil surface or mountainous granite domes such as Stone Mountain, which rises over 200 m (1,600 feet) above the surrounding area. These outcrops support unique plant communities and provide interesting examples of primary succession.

Succession begins when erosion forms depressions on the granite surface. The first organisms to colonize the depressions are lichens capable of surviving in the hot, dry environment of bare rock. As sand and organic material collect in the depressions, annuals such as stonecrop and reindeer moss that are able to grow in the thin soil colonize the area. As the soil layer thickens, true mosses and annual herbs establish. Perennial herbs and grasses follow as the water holding capacity of the soil increases. Eventually, increased plant cover and accumulation of sufficient soil supports growth of woody perennials such as loblolly pine, eastern red cedar, and sparkleberry. The process of primary succession on granite outcrops is very slow—it has been estimated that it can take over 700 years to transition from bare granite to pine scrub.

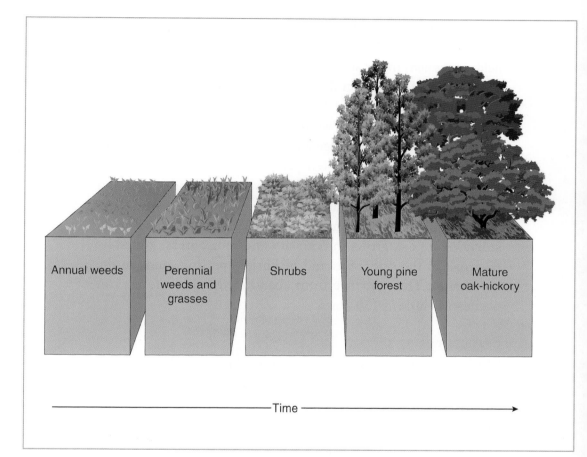

Figure 6.6 In secondary succession, a plant community is reestablished where the vegetation is disturbed but soil still remains. This process typically happens more quickly than primary succession.

secondary succession more than a less intense disturbance that damages only the plants.

The seral stages of secondary succession are familiar to anyone who has watched an area where the vegetation has been cleared. First, annual plants and weedy species establish on the site. These plants are followed by herbaceous perennial species and various shrubs. Early successional trees establish next and are ultimately replaced by later succesional species.

One of the best studied examples of secondary succession is that which occurs in abandoned agricultural areas (called **old-field succession**) in the southeastern United States. The sequence begins in the fall when crabgrass and horseweed establish in an abandoned field after the last crop has been harvested. After approximately two years, white aster and ragweed replace the initial colonists. Broomsedge and pine seedlings are the next to establish, and after about ten years, the site is dominated by young pine saplings. Shortleaf pines will grow on dry sites and loblolly pines on moist sites. Over the next 50 years, the pines mature and shade-tolerant hardwoods establish in the understory. White oak grows in both dry and moist areas, joined by post oak in the drier sites and hickories and dogwoods in the moist sites. The sequence from abandoned field to forest can occur in as little as 150 years.

CHANGES DURING SUCCESSION

Throughout the course of succession, there are characteristic changes in the community and ecosystem. For example, early in succession the environment is more extreme, much warmer and drier than in later successional stages. Nutrients are primarily stored in the soil and cycle more rapidly in early stages. In later seral stages, nutrients are stored in the plants and cycle much more slowly.

It is not just the abiotic environment that differs, but also the characteristics of the plants themselves. Early successional species are small, rapid-growing plants that tend to be r-strategists. Later successional species are typically large, slow-growing K-strategists. Early successional communities are often less complex than the later climax communities (see "Old Growth" box).

FORCES DRIVING SUCCESSION

Given that there are clearly definable stages in succession and obvious differences in the community and ecosystem, it is important to consider what forces cause these changes. Succession is driven by changes in the environment caused by organisms themselves. In the case of old-field succession described above, horseweed leaves contain allelopathic chemicals that inhibit the germination of horseweed seeds. Thus, these plants change the environment to inhibit their own presence. Succession can also be

Old Growth

One type of successional community that receives a great deal of attention is **old growth forests**. Old growth is a seral stage of forest succession that is beyond the climax stage. Old growth forests are comprised of trees that are older than the typical life span for the dominant species in an area. For example, the average age for Douglas fir is approximately 400 years, but old growth Douglas fir forests are composed of trees that are well over 750 years of age.

Old growth forests are more than just extremely old trees—they also have unique characteristics and relationships with other organisms in the community. Old growth forests contain trees that display the vicissitudes of age, such as broken crowns and damaged trunks, features that provide unique habitat for other species. For example, the northern spotted owl requires the hollow trunks of old growth trees for nesting sites. Other species of birds, insects, and fungi likewise require the unique conditions found only in very old trees for food and shelter. This is the key element of old growth forests: they provide a habitat that supports intricate webs of interacting species that cannot exist in even climax communities.

Unfortunately, old growth forests are now extremely rare. Forestry practices in the past, which focused on harvesting the largest and oldest individuals, have decimated these forests. Even today, timber companies fight for access to these ancient communities. Only through continued vigilance and protection can these forests continue to exist and house the species that depend on them.

driven by abiotic forces outside the organisms such as climate change. The forests that once dominated interior regions of the continents in the past were slowly replaced by extensive grasslands as the climate cooled and the areas became drier.

Different mechanisms have been identified that cause changes in a plant community during succession. Tolerance is one mechanism that shapes community composition. Their differing abilities to tolerate dissimilar conditions cause some species to appear and others to disappear in the community as the environment changes over succession. Thus, some organisms can tolerate pioneer conditions while a different group of organisms can tolerate climax conditions. Community composition is also shaped through facilitation and inhibition. Facilitation occurs as plants change environmental conditions that favor the growth of other species. Inhibition is due to changes in the environment that prevents establishment of individuals in the same or different species. For example, in old-field succession, pines create a shady, moist environment in the understory that inhibits establishment of their shade-intolerant offspring, but facilitates the establishment of shade-tolerant oak and hickory saplings.

Summary

Although they may appear to be static and unchanging, healthy plant communities are often in a dynamic state of change. Dramatic changes in plant communities may be due to disturbances that disrupt the vegetation. Of the many different forms of disturbance, fire has been particularly important in the evolution of species and the shaping of biome attributes. Changes in vegetation over time are called succession. Primary succession is a slow process that occurs on bare surfaces, and secondary succession is the relatively faster process that occurs on sites where the vegetation has been disturbed. The changes in community composition and ecosystem processes that occur over succession are due to changes in the environment. These changes are caused by the organisms themselves as well as outside forces. Although disturbance is often mistakenly viewed as a detrimental force in nature, it is essential in maintaining ecosystem health and promoting species diversity.

7 Plant Reproduction

The flower is the poetry of reproduction.
It is an example of the eternal seductiveness of life.

— Jean Giraudoux,
The Enchanted, 1933

Plant Reproduction

Flowers have been admired by humans throughout history: roses for their scent, tulips for their color, orchids for their shape. Gardeners around the world cultivate hundreds of species in endless variety. There are, however, some kinds of flowers that few people would consider attractive and fewer still would care to have in their gardens. Only certain insects truly appreciate the rotten perfume of carrion flowers. Such flowers mimic the appearance and stench of decaying flesh in order to attract insects for **pollination**. Flies and beetles that normally feed on and lay their eggs in the bodies of dead animals are "tricked" into visiting these flowers, thus perpetuating this bizarre, yet intriguing, reproductive strategy.

Reproduction is an essential component in the life cycle of all organisms. Like animals, plants have **sexual reproduction** in which sperm and egg unite to form offspring. In mosses and ferns, sperm swim from the male structures to the female structures to **fertilize** the egg. Gymnosperms and angiosperms package sperm in **pollen,** which is deposited on female structures of **cones** or flowers for pollination and fertilization.

In gymnosperm pollination, pollen is blown from male cones to female cones that secrete droplets of water from small openings to catch the pollen. When the droplet is drawn into the cone, the pollen germinates and forms a **pollen tube** that grows toward the egg and then releases the sperm to fertilize the egg. Fertilized eggs become embryos.

In angiosperms, pollen is produced in the **anther** of a flower. Pollination occurs when pollen lands on the **stigma** of the same or a different flower. The pollen grain then germinates to produce a pollen tube that grows through the **style** and into the **ovary**. Inside the ovary, the pollen tube grows toward the egg, releases the sperm, and fertilizes the egg. Fertilized eggs become embryos in **seeds** that are contained within fruits (see "Vegetative Reproduction" box).

Some plants depend on animals to transport pollen between flowers, while other plants use wind or water to transfer pollen.

Regardless of whether living or nonliving mechanisms are used, plants require specific structural features for effective pollination and fertilization (Table 7.1).

FLOWER COLOR AND SCENT

Their exceptional ability to attract pollinators makes flowers an important trait in the evolution of a very successful group of plants called angiosperms. Bright coloration of **petals, tepals**, or **bracts** in a single flower or a larger, multi-flowered **inflorescence** provides important visual cues to attract animal pollinators (Figure 7.1).

Because of differences in their eyes, not all animals perceive colors the same way and, therefore, are attracted to different colors. For example, flowers pollinated by bees, butterflies, and birds tend to be brightly colored. Beetle-pollinated flowers tend to have drab or dull coloration. Flowers pollinated by bats or moths tend to be pale or white and are easily visible at night when these nocturnal pollinators are active.

Vegetative Reproduction

Most plants reproduce sexually by producing seeds. However many plants do not completely depend on seeds for reproduction. Rather than investing all reproductive resources into seeds, some plants rely on **vegetative (asexual) reproduction** to produce exact copies of themselves. Irises, strawberries, and grasses are common examples of plants that reproduce vegetatively via **runners**, **rhizomes**, and **stolons**. Bamboos, in particular, rely heavily on vegetative reproduction. Bamboo species flower and produce seeds irregularly and infrequently, once every 100 years for some species. Therefore, they depend upon shoots produced from underground stem growth to increase the size of the plant and maintain dense populations.

Table 7.1 Characteristics of Flowers Pollinated by Different Mechanisms

POLLINATOR	PETAL COLOR/ PATTERNS	SCENT	SHAPE
Bats	Dull whites and greens	Strong fermented scent	Brush- or bowl-shaped
Bees	White, yellow, blue, purple, some reds, nectar guides common	Sweet scent	Bowl-shaped or tubular, often with "flag" or landing platform
Beetles	White, brownish	Strong sweet scent or fruit odors	Bowl-shaped
Birds	Bright red or orange	None	Deep, wide tube or brush-shaped
Butterflies	Blue, purple, pink, yellow, nectar guides	Moderately strong, sweet scent	Brush-shaped or with deep tubes and spurs
Carrion and dung flies	Brown, green, or dark red	Strong, foul scent	Open bowl-shaped
Flies	White or brown	None or weakly scented	Open bowl- or bell-shaped
Moths	White or drab colors	Strong scents, often sweet	Brush-shaped or with deep tubes and spurs
Wind	No specific coloration	None	Petals typically absent or very small, flowers in open dangling inflorescences, elaborate stigmas

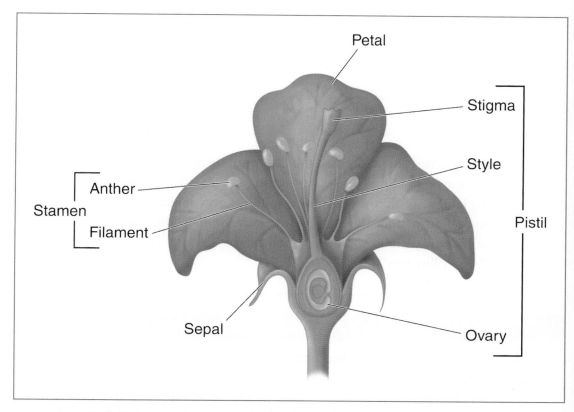

Figure 7.1 Flowers use color, scent, and shape to attract pollinators to the stamen, where pollen is produced, and the stigma, the receptive area where pollen grains germinate.

Petals can also have patterns of contrasting colors that direct pollinators into the flower and indicate where a reward might be hidden. Bees and other insects are also able to see not only the visible spectrum, but also ultraviolet wavelengths. Thus, petals that appear to be quite plain to a human might actually look like a well-lighted airport runway to an insect.

In addition to color, flowers use scent to attract pollinators. As mentioned above, bat-pollinated flowers tend to have pale coloration, but even a white flower can be difficult to see in the dark. Thus, bat- and moth-pollinated flowers also have strong, sweet, or musky odors that attract their pollinators. Bee- and butterfly-pollinated flowers tend to have sweeter fragrances, while bird-pollinated flowers have none at all (birds have no sense of smell).

FLOWER SHAPE

Flower shape also attracts pollinators. Petals can look like flag-like structures that capture the attention of pollinators. Petals can also be modified into platforms or perches where pollinators can land once they are attracted to the flower (Figure 7.2). But beyond attraction, floral shape dictates the mechanics of how pollinators pick up and deposit pollen (see "Flowers That Mimic Their Pollinators" box, Figure 7.2).

Flowers That Mimic Their Pollinators

There is no better example of the interaction between color, scent, and shape in plant reproduction than certain orchids whose flowers mimic the bees or wasps that pollinate them. Orchids in the genera *Ophrys* and *Drakea* have evolved color and petal shape modifications that cause the flowers to resemble the females of a particular wasp or bee species. The scent of the flowers completes the deception by mimicking the pheromone that the female insects release to attract mates.

These flowers are produced during periods when males far outnumber females, making them even more attractive to males, who visit and attempt to mate with the flower, a process known as **pseudocopulation**. During this process, pollen becomes attached to the insect's body.

Fooling the insect once is not enough, however. For pollination to occur, the male must attempt to mate with another flower, depositing the pollen on the stigma of this second flower. Thus, by exploiting the insect's instinct to reproduce, the plant ensures its own reproductive success without even offering a reward.

Figure 7.2 Flower shape is used to attract pollinators. Here, the flowers of an orchid resemble the female members of the bee species that pollinate them.

Some flowers have bell- or funnel-shaped flowers that insect pollinators crawl into and, in doing so, are dusted with pollen. Other plants have large, bowl-shaped flowers that coat the heads and bodies of the animals that visit them. Still other plants have trigger mechanisms that release pollen when they are tripped by an unsuspecting pollinator. Regardless of its shape or structure, each flower must achieve the same goal: to deposit pollen on and to remove pollen from a pollinator.

The process of depositing and removing pollen can be extremely complicated. For example, milkweeds have structurally complex flowers. Insect pollinators must first drag their leg through a groove on the flower where packets of pollen are attached to the insect's leg. The insect must then visit a flower on a different plant and again drag its leg through a groove where the pollen packets are removed from its leg and attached to the stigma (Figure 7.3).

Flower shape can also indicate coevolved mutualisms between a plant and its pollinators. Several Hawaiian lobelias have deep, curved, tubular flowers. The shapes of these flowers match the length and curvature of the beaks of the birds (honeycreepers) that pollinate them. Each plant species is pollinated by one type of honeycreeper: when a bird inserts its beak into a flower, it receives a dusting of pollen on its head; when it visits another flower, a stigma touches the bird's head, completing pollination. Such coevolved relationships, where the features of a flower correspond to the structural features of the pollinator, ensure that pollen will be transported between flowers of the same species, improving reproductive success for the plant.

POLLINATORS EXPECT A REWARD

While there are many ways for a plant to attract a pollinator, the question still remains: why would a pollinator visit the flower? Why, for example, would a honeycreeper want to repeatedly visit

Figure 7.3 Milkweed pollen is attached to the leg of a butterfly. Insect pollinators must drag their legs through a groove on the milkweed flower to pick up the pollen, then perform the same process to deposit it on another milkweed plant.

lobelia flowers? The answer is that the pollinator wants something, often food. In some plants, pollen itself is the reward. Pollen is thought to have been the first food reward offered to pollinators by the earliest angiosperms and insect-pollinated gymnosperms. Offering pollen as a reward, however, presents a conflict for the plant in that valuable pollen grains needed for reproduction are lost when the pollinator eats them. To offset this loss, plants that offer pollen as a reward must produce large quantities of energetically expensive pollen.

As a solution to the predicament of using pollen as a reward, some plants offer **nectar** instead. Nectar is a watery liquid containing sugars and other nutrients. Many species offer their reward in a relatively general manner, thereby allowing more than one species to act as a pollinator. Plants cannot afford, however, to offer their nectar openly to any passing animal. They need some assurance that only those pollinators who reliably pick up and deliver pollen to the appropriate locations receive this payment for services. So, nectar-producing structures are often hidden at the base of the flower, causing pollinators to probe the flower and come in contact with the stamens and stigma. Plants such as phlox, columbines, and lobelias produce and hold nectar in deep tube-shaped flowers or in special structures called **spurs** that can only be accessed by pollinators with the correct feeding structures (Figure 7.4). Despite the plants' best efforts to reserve nectar for the correct pollinators, some insects called **nectar robbers** are still able to access nectar (either through existing openings or by poking a hole in the flower) without providing any pollination services in return (see "Specialization in Columbines" box).

ABIOTIC POLLINATION

Though animals can be quite useful in transporting pollen, many plants do not depend on them at all for reproduction.

Wind is the most common abiotic means to transport pollen in gymnosperms and angiosperms. As with animal-pollinated plants, wind-pollinated plants require specific structural features for successful reproduction.

In gymnosperms, cones rather than flowers are used for reproduction. Many common gymnosperms, such as pines, spruces, and firs, produce pollen in small, papery male cones. Pollen grains in these species have small air sacs that help the pollen float in the air. In wind-pollinated angiosperms such as grasses or oaks, flowers have highly reduced petals or may lack petals completely. Furthermore, these flowers bear their anthers in loose, open inflorescences that release pollen easily in a breeze (Figure 7.5).

While releasing pollen is relatively easy for a wind-pollinated species, catching pollen carried on a breeze is much more

(continued on page 108)

Specialization in Columbines

Flowers have combinations of traits that are suited for particular pollinators. Slight variations in these traits can change how the flowers are pollinated and, consequently, what animals will visit them. Columbines are a common type of flower in the Rocky Mountains of North America. These flowers offer nectar in spurs as a reward for their pollinators. Western columbine has downward hanging red flowers with relatively short spurs. Hummingbirds approach the flowers from below and hover under the flowers. Pollen is deposited on the bird's head as it drinks nectar from the spurs. The Sierra columbine often grows near western columbine. This species has erect white flowers with deep spurs. Moths attracted to these flowers are the only animals able to access the nectar because only their long mouth parts can reach deep enough into the spur. Thus, although the flowers of these related species have many similar features, their differences are suited to visits by very different pollinators.

Figure 7.4 The bird-pollinated western columbine (A) and the moth-pollinated Sierra columbine (B) hold nectar in deep tube-shaped flowers that can only be accessed by particular pollinators.

Figure 7.5 Many common gymnosperms such as spruce (Picea) produce pollen in small, papery male cones (A, B) for wind dispersal. The catkins of the Coastal Plain Willow (*Salix cardiniana*) (C) release pollen easily in a breeze.

(continued from page 105)

difficult. Without a pollinator to specifically deposit pollen in the appropriate location, wind pollination depends, to some extent, on chance. To improve their odds of locating and depositing pollen on the cone or stigma of the same species, wind-pollinated species must produce large quantities of pollen. Specialization of female structures also improves the probability of pollen landing in the right place. For example, grass flowers typically have feathery stigmas that increase the surface area for pollen to land upon. Female cones on pines and other gymnosperms have aerodynamic properties that produce patterns of wind flow to direct pollen toward the receptive female structures.

Water pollination is quite rare in angiosperms. In species such as ribbon weed or water celery, pollen floats from male to female flowers borne on the surface of the water. Water is a much more common component in the reproduction of ferns and mosses. In these plants, sperm cells swim, following chemical signals, to locate and fertilize the egg. This dependence on water for reproduction is one of several factors restricting ferns, mosses, and related plants to moist habitats.

Summary

Reproduction is an important process requiring plants to interact with their environment. Regardless of whether biotic or abiotic mechanisms are used for reproduction, modifications of flowers, cones, or other reproductive structures are necessary to successfully unite sperm and egg. These modifications reflect the particular characteristics and behaviors of the pollination mechanism. Animal-pollinated plants use combinations of traits such as color, scent, and shape to attract the attention of pollinators. In contrast, wind-pollinated plants have reduced petals because pollinator attraction is not necessary. They also have traits that enable pollen to be picked up and carried by the wind. Animal-pollinated plants must expend energy to reward pollinators in order to promote visitation. Wind-pollinated plants, on the other hand, must expend energy to produce large quantities of pollen to increase the probability of successful reproduction.

8 How Plants Disperse

Many things grow in the garden
that were never sown there.

— Thomas Fuller,
Gnomologia, 1732

How Plants Disperse

In the science fiction classic *The Day of the Triffids*, humankind is plagued by plants that can walk and move across the landscape at will. While there is no such thing as walking plants, it is wrong to consider plants completely immobile. Although individual plants are literally rooted in place, they do move from location to location in a series of steps from parent to offspring. Consider a hillside that has been cleared of plants after a fire, a tended field that has had all vegetation removed, or a sandbar scoured clean after a flood. No plants are present. Yet, over time, plant species appear and begin to populate the area. Some were brought to these locations as seeds from plants growing elsewhere. Others were here all along, lying dormant in the soil until the environment cued them to germinate and grow. Therefore, though they do not move in the animal sense, plants have evolved the ability to travel from place to place and from the present to the future.

DISPERSAL AND GERMINATION

After reproducing, the plant must disperse its offspring to **safe sites** that are suitable for **germination** and establishment of new plants. Because plants cannot actively seek out safe sites, they must use structural and physiological adaptations to disperse seeds or spores.

Many species release their seed and saturate the area around the maternal plant to secure it for the plant's future offspring. However, because many offspring from the same parent will be deposited in close proximity to one another, localized dispersal alone can lead to intense competition among related individuals, which may reduce the number of descendants that survive from the parent. Limited dispersal can also lead to competition between a larger parent plant and its offspring. For example, a tree can produce hundreds of seeds each year, but due to shading under the parent, few offspring may be able to establish and thrive as long as the parent plant dominates the site. An additional consideration is that while the site where the parent plant is growing may have been a safe site in the past, environmental conditions may have changed over the course of succession so that it is no longer suitable for that species. To avoid these potential risks of local dispersal, mechanisms have evolved to carry seeds away from the parent plant, reducing competition among siblings and promoting colonization of new sites.

ABIOTIC DISPERSAL

While no special features are required for a seed to fall from the parent plant, there are many different structural modifications of seeds and fruits that influence how the seeds are released and fall to the ground. In plants such as poppies, seeds are shaken from the fruit (a **capsule** in this case) like salt from a shaker as the plant sways in the breeze. In moss capsules and in fruits of angiosperms such as wood sorrel, vetch, and maypop, pressure develops within the fruiting structure which, when released, hurls the seeds or spores several meters from the parent plant (Figure 8.1).

Another common form of abiotic seed dispersal in both gymnosperms and angiosperms is wind dispersal (**anemochory**). In plants with this dispersal strategy, fruits of the seeds themselves have structural modifications that allow the seed to be carried on wind currents. One such modification is the wing structure on the seeds of pines or the **samara** fruits of maples. The shape and size of the wing cause the seed to spin as it falls, spiraling away from the parent plant. Dandelions and other members of the sunflower family have a **pappus** attached to each fruit, which acts like a parachute to lift the fruit into the air and carry it away. Milkweeds use a similar strategy with a tuft of hair attached to each seed that carries it away when the fruit is ripe. While these examples show how structures can be modified to aid in wind dispersal, some species have no specific modifications beyond size. Many orchids have seeds so small that they are

Figure 8.1 In plants such as poppy, seeds are shaken from the fruit (a capsule) as the plant sways in the breeze.

referred to as dust seeds, and indeed they are dispersed on the wind like blowing dust. In some cases, the entire plant is a dispersal unit. Tumbleweeds ripen their fruit on the plant and then the plant stem breaks at ground level. As the wind blows the entire plant across the landscape, seeds are jostled out of the fruits and dropped along the way.

Water can also be an effective dispersal medium (**hydrochory**). Some of the best examples of this dispersal strategy are tropical island and coastal species such as coconut palms. The large, round seed is encased in a buoyant, fibrous husk. These fruits can be picked up by tides and carried on ocean currents. The water softens the husks so that the seeds are ready to germinate when they wash up on distant shores. Many other **riparian** and wetland species such as cottonwood, willow, and alder drop their seeds in lakes, rivers, or streams, where they are carried on the water to safe sites along the shoreline.

ANIMAL DISPERSAL

While abiotic factors such as wind and water can be very effective for seed dispersal, some plants enlist the aid of animals to transport seeds (**zoochory**). As with abiotic dispersal, biotic dispersal usually requires specific structural modifications of the fruit or seed. The nature of the modifications, however, depends on whether the animal is an unsuspecting participant in seed dispersal or is being enticed and rewarded for its services (see "Ants and Plants" box).

Ants and Plants

Birds and mammals are not the only animals capable of dispersing seeds—ants, too, can be effective agents of seed dispersal. Relative to their body size, ants are some of the strongest animals on Earth, capable of lifting and moving objects that are much larger than themselves. Some plants exploit the strength of ants, depending on these tiny animals to disperse their seeds.

Some plants produce seeds that have a small structure called an **elaiosome** attached. The elaiosome is rich in lipids and sterols that the ants require in their diet. The ants collect the seed and take it back to their nest, where they feed the elaiosome to their larvae and place the seed in an underground waste area. Hidden from aboveground predators, the seed germinates and grows strong in the nitrogen and phosphorus-rich waste.

Ectozoochory involves attaching a seed to the outside of an animal. One way that seeds can be attached is through the production of hooks or barbs on the outside of the fruit (Figure 8.2). Species such as Spanish needles, beggars lice, cocklebur, and needle grass will attach to the fur of animals that brush against the plant. The seed will either fall off or be groomed off of the animal at a later time. Dwarf mistletoes are parasitic plants of trees such as ponderosa pine and lodgepole pine. Dwarf mistletoe seeds are coated with a sticky substance that glues the seed to the feet or beaks of birds that pop their fruits. When the birds fly to another perch, the seeds become detached from the bird and stick to the branches of a new host tree.

Special adaptations are not always necessary for ectozoochory. Many aquatic and semiaquatic species that grow near bodies of water drop their seeds in the mud. Waterfowl walking through the mud will have the mud-seed mixture stick to their legs. When they travel to another pond or lake, the seeds are washed off in a new location.

Endozoochory is the transportation of seeds inside an animal. This type of dispersal presents a risk for the plant, which is literally offering some of its progeny as food. Seeds that are damaged in the digestive process will not survive to grow and reproduce. However, some seeds inevitably survive this internal journey to be deposited at a distance from the parent plant, with the added bonus of a healthy dose of fertilizer.

When using endozoochory, however, it is important for the plant to be able to signal to animals when the fruit is ready to be eaten. If the fruit is eaten before it is ripe, the seeds inside it may not be mature enough to germinate. Thus, immature fruits are often green to hide them from animals. When they ripen, their color change attracts potential dispersers. For example, fruits of the tropical tree aguacatillo are a dark green color and are attached to the tree by a light green cupule. This coloration camouflages the immature fruit against the green background of

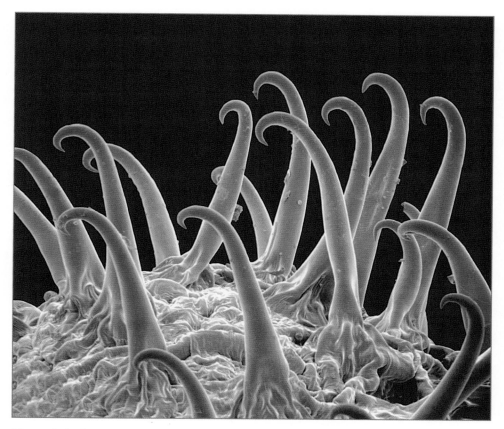

Figure 8.2 To facilitate dispersal, the cocklebur fruit is covered with hooks to attach to the fur of animals that brush against the plant.

the forest (Figure 8.3). However, as it matures, the fruit turns black and the cupule turns a brilliant red. The new coloration pattern is highly visible to birds such as resplendent quetzals and emerald toucanettes. These birds swallow the fruits whole, fly to another site to digest the lipid-rich fruit layer, and then regurgitate the seed.

The orientation of a seed, or how it is presented to an animal, may also increase its visibility. For example, in most pine species, the female seed-bearing cones hang downward, allowing their seeds to be dispersed by gravity and wind. Cones of the

Figure 8.3 The aguacatillo tree fruits change colors to attract birds to ingest them. The birds then disperse the seeds to another site. The transportation of seeds inside an animal is called endozoochory.

whitebark pine, in contrast, point upwards. The upward orientation prevents the seeds from simply falling to the ground and makes them more visible to birds such as Clark's nutcracker (Figure 8.4). Birds gather several seeds from a cone into a pouch in their throat and then fly to open, treeless sites, where they bury the seeds for eating at a later time. Uneaten seeds may germinate to establish new plants.

SEEDS NEED STIMULI TO GERMINATE
Dispersal is only the first step in establishing offspring. Once a seed has been transported, it must then be stimulated to germinate and grow (see "Heterocarpy and Ecological Bet Hedging" box),

Figure 8.4 Whitebark pines hold their cones upward to prevent the seeds from falling out and to attract Clark's nutcrackers to extract them.

(Figure 8.5). Germination is often linked to specific environmental cues that indicate when conditions are appropriate for establishment and growth of a particular species. Water, temperature, and light are the main factors that influence germination.

Water may be the most important stimulus for germination. The plant embryo is dormant partly due to lack of water within the seed. When water is absorbed by a seed, enzymes are activated that reinitiate embryo growth and development. Likewise, some seeds contain chemicals that inhibit germination. Repeated washing of the seed by soil water rinses these chemicals from the seeds and allows germination. The necessity for the inhibitor to be washed from the seed prevents the seed from germinating immediately in response to the presence of water but rather delays germination until there is sufficient water available for the young plant.

Temperature is another important germination regulator. Species in different habitats often have different temperature requirements for germination, but, in general, germination rates

Heterocarpy and Ecological Bet Hedging

In most angiosperms, all fruits produced by an individual plant are structurally and functionally identical. In a few species, however, different flowers on the same plant produce two or more distinct types of fruits, a phenomenon known as **heterocarpy**. Heterocarpy is particularly common in the sunflower family. The single "sunflower" is actually an inflorescence of many small **florets**. Each floret can produce a fruit (**achene**) containing a single seed. In heterocarpic species, achenes produced by florets in the central region of the inflorescence are small, have structures to promote distant dispersal, and germinate immediately. In contrast, achenes produced by peripherally positioned florets are large, lack dispersal structures, and have dormancy mechanisms that prevent germination until a later time (Figure 8.5).

Heterocarpic plants are often early colonists of unpredictable, disturbed habitats. Disturbed sites also undergo succession, which ultimately makes the site unsuitable for the early colonists. By producing different types of fruits, plants of heterocarpic species help maintain the existing population and colonize new sites at the same time. Thus, by combining different dispersal and dormancy traits in their offspring, a plant can survive a wider range of environmental conditions as well as cycles of population colonization and extinction, and ultimately maintain high reproductive success in light of unpredictable environmental variations.

Figure 8.5 In a few species of plants, different flowers on the same plant produce distinct types of fruits, a phenomenon known as heterocarpy. This strategy is useful to plants in disturbed habitats. Here, we see the heterocarpous fruits of *Grindelia ciliata*.

are higher at warm temperatures than cool temperatures. However, the relationship between temperature and germination can be more complex than what is simply the optimal germination temperature. For example, in winter annual species, seeds germinate when the temperature is below a particular maximum. Thus, these species germinate in the fall or winter and then flower and set seed in the following spring. Their seeds then remain dormant in the soil throughout the summer until the temperature drops. In contrast, seeds of summer annuals do not germinate unless temperature is above a particular minimum. These plants germinate in the spring or summer and then flower in summer or fall. Their seeds are dispersed in the fall and are dormant throughout the winter. It is not always a constant temperature that stimulates germination but rather the range of temperatures a seed experiences between day and night that stimulates growth. Such dependence on temperature fluctuations is an effective indicator of seasonal change and environmental conditions (see "Oldest Germinated Seeds" box).

Specific temperature regimes can also be required to break dormancy. Seeds of some plants that grow at temperate and higher latitudes require **stratification**, the exposure of seeds to moisture followed by a period of cold temperatures, before they

Oldest Germinated Seeds

Through dormancy, a seed can postpone germination until some time in the future when environmental cues allow germination to begin. Over time, dormant seeds can lose their viability, which has led researchers to investigate how long a seed can remain viable. In one study, seeds from 23 species were buried for 100 years and seeds from three annuals were still able to germinate. Other studies have discovered a similar trend that small seeds from annuals and weedy plants tend to retain viability in the soil for long periods of time, greater than 50 years in many instances. Trees and other long-lived perennials tend to produce larger seeds that have shorter viability, often less than five years. Seeds from aquatic habitats tend to retain viability for long periods of time as well, because the cool, damp environment in mud sediments has a preserving effect that inhibits seed death and decay.

Seeds of the sacred lotus are the oldest ever germinated. The seeds were collected from deposits in a lake bed in Pulantien, China. After lying dormant for 1,288 years, the oldest seed germinated in less than four days. A second seed, aged at 684 years, likewise germinated quickly. Unfortunately, to determine the age of the seeds through radiocarbon methods, the seedlings had to be incinerated immediately before they incorporated present-day carbon into their tissues.

are able to respond to other environmental stimuli and germinate. Stratification prevents seeds from germinating until after the winter season has passed.

Light is the final stimulus required for germination. In some seeds, germination inhibitors are present that degrade when exposed to light. In other species, germination is optimal after exposure to certain combinations of light-dark (**photoperiods)** that are indicative of seasonal changes.

Other factors can also be important regulators of germination. In some seeds, a tough, impervious **seed coat** around the seed can prevent germination. Through **scarification**, a physical or chemical weakening of the seed coat, seeds are then able to germinate. Scarification can occur through physical abrasion in the soil or repeated freeze-thaw cycles. Plants in fire-prone biomes such as the chaparral have also evolved a dependence on fire to heat and crack the seed coat. A seed may also be scarified as it passes through an animal's digestive tract. The acidic environment of the stomach weakens the seed coat so that dormancy is broken by the time the seed passes through the animal.

Summary

Plants must disperse spores or seeds to new sites in order to establish new plants. Spores and seeds can be dispersed through abiotic or biotic means. Abiotic dispersal depends upon gravity, wind, or water, while biotic dispersal relies on animals to transport seeds. Regardless of the dispersal vectors, specific physical features are required for the strategy to function effectively. Once dispersed, the spore or seed requires appropriate environmental conditions to germinate: water, temperature, and light can provide reliable indicators of germination. Thus, although a plant is immobile, a variety of structural and physiological mechanisms are used by plants to disperse their offspring in space and time.

9 The Impact of Agriculture

Ever since man began to till the soil and learned not to eat the seed grain but to plant it and wait for the harvest, the postponement of gratification has been the basis of a higher standard of living and civilization.

— S. I. Hayakawa (1906–1992)
U.S. scholar

The Impact of Agriculture

Twelve thousand years ago, humans in Asia, the Fertile Crescent, and Mesoamerica were beginning to learn that plants used for food or fibers could be grown by placing seeds in the ground. Scientists have proposed that planting seeds may have started by accident. Individuals in a population of hunter-gatherers may have noticed that useful plants could be found growing in the waste heaps near campsites where uneaten plant parts were tossed.

Agriculture did not establish immediately. A transitional period of thousands of years was necessary for human populations to gradually domesticate more and more wild plant species. Archaeological evidence indicates that by 10,000 years ago, agriculture was well established and the human population had begun to develop the food base that would support population growth.

Today, 15% of Earth's surface has been converted to agricultural areas and an additional 8% for pastures to feed livestock[2] (Figure 9.1). Modern agriculture supports a human population of over six billion people. Unfortunately, some agricultural practices can negatively impact the environment. **Sustainable agriculture** based on ecologically sound farming methods must be used to protect agricultural areas if they are to support the growing human population.

Although they are manmade, agroecosystems operate according to the same principles as natural communities and ecosystems. Energy flows and matter cycles according to the laws of thermodynamics and biogeochemistry. Individual organisms are subject to a variety of intraspecific and interspecific interactions. But, because they are structured and managed by humans, agroecosystems differ from natural ecosystems in how these phenomena occur.

MAJOR CROP SPECIES

The first domesticated crops were derived from native plant species. Wheat, barley, peas, and lentils in the Near East; rice and

126

Figure 9.1 Today, 15% of the Earth's surface has been converted to agriculture. Natural vegetation is cleared and replaced with one or more crop species.

millet in the Far East; and squash, avocado, beans, potatoes, and corn in the Americas. Though the species differed greatly from region to region, every culture also domesticated at least one grass that would serve as a staple of their diet.

Agronomists have studied the puzzle of the origins of different crop species. Not surprisingly, the origins for most major crops are located in species-rich tropical and subtropical regions (Figure 9.2). Many crops originated in an area where their taxonomic group is most diverse. Some crops (such as cotton) were domesticated independently in different places. Domesticated crops spread around the globe as cultures came into contact with one another.

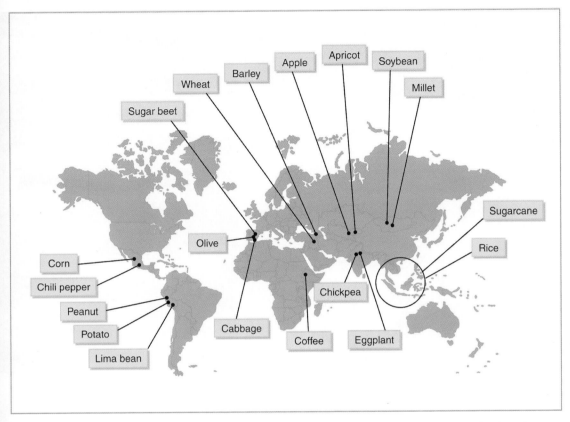

Figure 9.2 The origins for most major crops are located in species-rich tropical and subtropical regions of the world.

Of the more than 250,000 species of flowering plants, most agricultural activities are focused on just 20 species. A majority of crop species are in the grass family (Poaceae): wheat, rice, corn, barley, oats, sorghum, millet, rye, and sugarcane. Species in the bean family (legumes) comprise the next largest group with five major crops: soybeans, peanuts, field beans, chick peas, and pigeon peas. The remaining major crops—potatoes, sweet potatoes, cassavas, sugar beets, bananas, coconuts—come from a variety of other families. Three crops (corn, wheat, and rice) satisfy 90% of the world's food needs.

AGRICULTURE CHANGES VEGETATION

The primary impact of agriculture is extensive modification of habitat. Natural vegetation is cleared and replaced with one or several crop species. Removal of native vegetation not only simplifies the plant community, but it also has a cascade of effects on other organisms as well. Soil microorganisms, fungi, invertebrates, birds, mammals, and other organisms that depend on the natural vegetation for habitat and food are lost from the community. Thus, planting crops homogenizes the entire biological community and simplifies the ecosystem (Figure 9.3).

In large-scale farming, extensive areas are often covered by a single species, planted in orderly rows at a uniform density. This uniformity increases the efficiency of food production. However, because costly specialized machinery is necessary at all stages from planting through harvest, farmers must repeatedly grow the same crop in order to recover their equipment investment. Unfortunately, this repetitive planting strategy depletes the soil of nutrients required by that crop.

PLOWING DISTURBS SOIL

In addition to the biotic environment, agriculture significantly impacts the abiotic environment, particularly soil. Soil is the key to agriculture. Not only is it the matrix for anchoring plants, but soil also provides the mineral nutrition required for growth of vegetation. It likewise provides habitat for many of the organisms that are essential for ecosystem function. Yet, even though the importance of soil in agriculture is clearly understood, some agricultural practices damage soil, making it necessary to understand these impacts in order to develop more effective farming methods.

Tillage, the process of working soil to make it suitable for growing crops, has the most obvious and dramatic impact on soil. Conventional tillage methods use plowing, disking, and other forms of soil treatment to thoroughly prepare the seedbed

Figure 9.3 In large-scale farming, extensive areas are often covered by a single species (monoculture). This planting strategy depletes the soil of nutrients.

for crops by breaking-up and homogenizing the soil. Soil quality is increased somewhat when crop residues are plowed under, contributing to the organic content of the soil as they decompose. Nutrients that have leached into lower soil layers are redistributed into upper layers. Plowing and disking also aid in weed control by killing undesirable plants and disrupting their soil seed bank.

However, tillage does have detrimental impacts on soil and agroecosystems. By removing the protective cover of vegetation, soil is susceptible to **erosion**, which removes fertile upper layers of soil, exposing infertile lower layers. Water erosion washes fine soil particles and organic material into reservoirs and waterways, where they are of no use for agriculture. Soils without vegetative cover are also susceptible to wind erosion, which blows away upper soil layers. One of the most devastating examples of wind erosion occurred in the Great Plains of North America during the 1930s when extensive plowing and record drought left soil exposed to dust storms that blew away tons of soil and devastated over 83 million acres of farmland.[3] It is estimated that erosion results in a worldwide loss of 28 billion tons of soil each year and a reduction in arable farmland at the rate of approximately 1% per year.

Soil can be protected against erosion through modified approaches to the way in which soil is treated. **Reduced tillage** methods reduce the number of times soil is disrupted as well as the extent of plowing so that some of the soil in a field is not disturbed. **No tillage** approaches do not disturb the soil at all except to plant seeds. Both of these methods allow some of the residues from previous crops to remain in place and protect the soil. Modified approaches to planting also protect against erosion. Terracing can be used on steep slopes to reduce erosion by slowing the rate of water movement down the slope. Contour plowing follows natural contours on the land to reduce rates of water flow down slopes. Contour plowing can be particularly effective when combined with strip farming. In strip farming, crops which can grow in high densities such as wheat are alternated between strips of crops that grow in more regular rows such as corn or soybeans. Crops grown at high densities slow the rate of water movement down a slope and reduce erosion in areas where greater spacing between plants exposes more soil.

FERTILIZER ALTERS NUTRIENT CYCLES

A second impact of agriculture on soil is through the application of fertilizers. Natural soil nutrients may be lost through erosion or through the practice of growing the same crop repeatedly. These soil nutritional losses may be offset by the application of fertilizers.

Many gains in crop production in the past 50 years have been due to fertilizers. Following World War II, organizations such as the Ford and Rockefeller Foundations as well as various governmental agencies around the world set up research systems to breed better crops of species such as wheat and rice. These intensive research efforts, hailed as the "Green Revolution," developed varieties of crops that had higher food yields. These new varieties required more fertilizer and water to achieve the increased yield. While the benefits of increased yield are obvious, excessive use and dependence on fertilizers and other agrochemicals do present problems. Economically, fertilizers are expensive and difficult for smaller farms to afford, making it even less likely that they will be able to compete with larger farming operations. Fertilizers are also energy intensive to produce and they are often derived from petroleum, a non-renewable resource.

Another problem associated with fertilizers is that they do not stay in place after they are applied. Fertilizers can leach from the soil and wash into waterways. The resulting nutrient enrichment of water can promote explosive growth of algae, polluting and reducing water quality.

Crop rotation can be used to decrease the need to enhance soil nutrient content with fertilizers. In crop rotation, nitrogen-fixing cover crops such as alfalfa, clover, or soybeans are planted in a field for several years. These plants have symbiotic, nitrogen-fixing bacteria in their roots, so these crops will accumulate high levels of nitrogen in their roots and stems. After growing for one to two years, the cover crop is plowed under, which increases soil nitrogen content and adds organic material to the soil, increasing soil water-holding capacity (Figure 9.4). Next, a cash crop such as corn is grown in the field for several years, and then the cover crop is grown again. Crop rotation uses natural processes of nitrogen uptake and decomposition to improve soil quality.

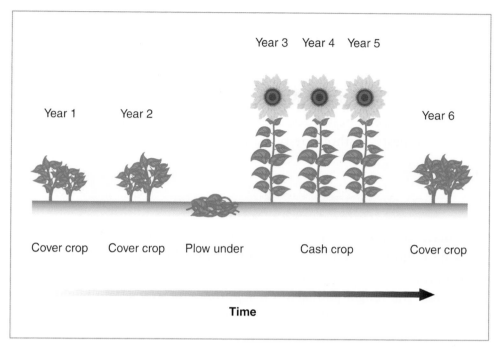

Figure 9.4 In crop rotation, nitrogen-fixing crops are grown and then plowed under to increase soil nutrients and water-holding capacity. The cash crop is grown in the field for several years, and then the cover crop is grown again.

PESTS AND PEST MANAGEMENT

The objective of an agricultural field is to grow food for humans. Unfortunately, insects, fungi, and other pests are also attracted to fields as a food source. A large monoculture of healthy crops provides a huge target for pest species. Crops within a monoculture are often genetically identical to one another, causing all individuals to be equally susceptible to pests. Thus, a pest invasion can quickly become a pest epidemic. Weeds can also act as pests, invading fields to compete with crops for space, nutrients, and water (see "Genetic Variation and the Irish Potato Famine" box).

To combat these species that come between humans and their crops, a variety of **pesticides** (fungicides, herbicides, insecticides) have been used for centuries. The Sumerians of 5,000 years ago and the Chinese of 2,500 years ago used sulfur, mercury, and arsenic to kill pests on crops. Modern pesticides utilize synthetic chemicals such as chlorinated hydrocarbons, carbamates, and organophosphates.

Pesticide use does protect crops to a certain extent, but even with the use of pesticides, 30% of all annual crop production is lost to pests. Without pesticides, this number would escalate to

Genetic Variation and the Irish Potato Famine

The potato became a staple in the diet of Irish peasants by the early 1600s, allowing rapid growth of the Irish population (from 1.5 million in 1760 to 8.5 million in 1840). But in the summer of 1845, the unimaginable happened. The fungal pathogen *Phytophthora infestans* (late blight) came to Ireland, speading rapidly in the cool, damp climate. Because the entire potato crop originated from one or two plants introduced to Ireland from South America, all plants were equally susceptible to the disease, allowing late blight to spread unchecked. The entire potato crop was devastated—in a matter of weeks, leaves blackened and decayed, and potatoes rotted in the ground. Over 1 million people died of starvation and at least 1.5 million Irish emigrated to other lands. Had the potato crop been more genetically variable, there may have been more differences in disease susceptibility among plants and the consequences might have been less devastating.

Although the Irish potato famine is undoubtedly the worst case, it is not the only example of such devastation. In the 1970s, corn leaf blight destroyed 15% of the U.S. corn crop (50% in some areas of the southern U.S.). Again, the crops were predominantly of a single genetic variety with equal susceptibility to the disease. If agronomists can identify wild relatives of crop species that are resistant to various diseases, they can potentially breed resistance into crops. However, as long as agriculture depends on growth of genetically uniform monocultures, the specter of crop devastation by a single pathogen will always be present.

unacceptable levels. However, these benefits must be considered in light of their negative impacts. Broad-spectrum pesticides kill not only pest species, but also desirable species. Another negative impact of pesticide use is the evolution of resistance to it by targeted pest species. By chance, some individuals in a pest species can contain genetic mutations that make them insensitive to the pesticide. If they survive and reproduce, pesticide resistance will spread to future pest generations rendering the pesticide useless. Yet another negative impact of pesticide use is that it can be incorporated into the food chain. Animals such as birds and even humans may accumulate harmful levels of pesticides in their bodies by consuming animals that have consumed insects which have, in turn, consumed the pesticides.

Integrated pest management uses ecological principles to reduce dependence on pesticides. For example, natural predators such as ladybird beetles are released into fields to prey on crop pests. Some plants such as marigolds produce pesticides naturally and can help to repel pests when planted alongside cash crops. Crop rotation also helps to manage pests by regularly depriving them of their food source, thus preventing their populations from growing too large. Use of these techniques as part of a comprehensive pest management plan that includes the careful application of pesticides can help protect food sources and reduce the environmental impacts of agriculture at the same time.

GENETIC ENGINEERING

The ability of scientists to manipulate DNA has allowed the development of **genetically modified organisms** (**GMOs**), which are increasingly becoming part of modern agriculture. Molecular biology has developed the tools whereby desirable genes can be identified in a species, cut from the DNA of that species, and then inserted into the DNA of a crop species. GMOs have been developed for a variety of crops including soybeans, corn, potatoes, tomatoes, cotton, wheat, and rice.

A variety of traits have been genetically engineered into GMOs. Two of the most common traits are for resistance to herbicides and insects. Resistance to the herbicide glyphosate has been introduced into crops using a gene from a bacterium. A gene from another soil bacterium, *Bacillus thuringiensis,* encodes for production of a protein toxic to insects (*Bt* toxin). It has been inserted into the DNA of crops such as potatoes and corn, making every cell of the crop plant capable of producing a pesticide that will kill insects that eat it. Genes to slow fruit ripening, increase vitamin content, improve drought tolerance, protect against freezing, and others have also been successfully introduced to crops.

While there are obvious benefits to the use of GMOs, they do present ecological concerns. For example, the impact of an increase in *Bt* toxin in the environment is not known. If crops modified for herbicide resistance are grown in the vicinity of related species that are weeds, then herbicide resistance could be transferred from the crop to wild populations. GMOs could also be dangerous to human health if allergens from one species are accidentally introduced into other foods. Therefore, although GMOs are certain to be part of agriculture in the future, continued scientific research is necessary to evaluate their ecological impact. Informed public discussion will also be necessary to determine whether and how this new agricultural technology should be applied (see "Golden Rice" box).

Summary

Agriculture has altered the natural landscape like no other human activity. Native vegetation is removed, alien species are introduced and planted in extensive monoculture, biogeochemical cycles are altered, and food webs are disrupted as a result of agriculture. There have been, and will continue to be, benefits from modern agricultural technology. However, some practices have detrimental impacts on the environment. In the future, agriculture must include sustainable practices in order to protect existing agricultural areas that are essential to feeding the growing human population.

Golden Rice

Rice is the most important staple crop in the world. Over two-thirds of the human population depends on agricultural production of two species, Asian rice (grown worldwide) and African rice (grown in regions of West Africa). The food sold as "wild rice" in North America is not rice at all, but is actually a cultivated species from a related genus.

Because of its importance in the human food chain, plant ecologists in the 1970s began collecting samples and studying the different varieties of cultivated species as well as the 20 different wild species. These different species and varieties are adapted to a wide range of local environmental conditions. Some grow well in full sun, while others perform better in shade. Some prefer wet, marshy conditions, while others prefer moderately dry soils. Species also differ in disease resistance. Given this tremendous diversity of traits, researchers are working to introduce traits such as disease resistance from wild species into the cultivated species to improve agricultural production.

"Golden rice" is the nickname of an important GMO. Genes from bacteria and daffodils that produce beta-carotene, a precursor for vitamin A in the body, have been inserted into the rice DNA. It is hoped that eating golden rice will reduce the occurrence of vision problems related to vitamin A deficiency, which plague many poor populations who depend on rice as their main food. While golden rice has obvious benefits, some have argued against it for several reasons: growing golden rice exclusively will increase the dependence of a large number of people on a single variety of this crop, a situation that could lead to a disaster like the Irish potato famine. Also, the long-term health effects of GMOs on humans are not known.

10 Conserving the Earth's Resources

I hope that while so many people are out smelling the flowers, someone is taking the time to plant some.

— Herbert Rappaport

Conserving the Earth's Resources

"The tide of the Earth's population is rising, the reservoir of the Earth's living resources is falling. . . . Man must recognize the necessity of cooperating with nature. He must temper his demands and use and conserve the natural living resources of this Earth in a manner that alone can provide for the continuation of his civilization. The final answer is to be found only through comprehension of the enduring process of nature. The time for defiance is at an end."

These words, which sound as though they could have been written only yesterday, were written in 1948 by Fairfield Osborn in his book *Our Plundered Planet*.[4] Even then, scientists recognized that humans are having a dramatic and often detrimental impact on the Earth and its ecosystems. Humans have become a major ecological force on the planet. There is no part of the Earth system that is not impacted by the activities of humans. In some instances, the impacts are clearly evident, while in others the effects are less obvious. The field of conservation biology is focused on understanding the ecological basis of environmental problems faced by species and ecosystems in order to develop ecologically sound solutions. Its primary goals are to (1) protect species, (2) preserve genetic variation within species, (3) protect habitats and ecosystems, and (4) maintain ecological processes.

THE VALUE OF BIODIVERSITY

One of the greatest ecological threats caused by human activities is the rapid loss of **biodiversity**. The protection and maintenance of plant diversity is important for several reasons. First, plant diversity is a biological resource that humans have repeatedly turned to throughout their history. Wild plants have provided all of our existing crops and many more are being tried. Plants were the first source of medicines and continue to provide the raw materials for new pharmaceuticals. Approximately 25% of all prescription drugs contain chemicals extracted from plants.[5]

Rauvolfia
Rauvolfia sepentina
Southeast Asia
Tranquilizer, high blood
pressure medication

Foxglove
Digitalis purpurea
Europe
Digitalis for heart failure

Rosy periwinkle
Cathranthus roseus
Madagascar
Hodgkin's disease,
lymphocytic leukemia

Pacific Yew
Taxus brevifolia
Pacific Northwest
Ovarian cancer

Cinchona
Cinchona ledogeriana
South America
Quinine for malaria
treatment

Neem tree
Azadirachta indica
India
Treatment of many
diseases, insecticide,
spermicide

Figure 10.1 Plant biodiversity is important for several reasons, one of which is that plants provide the raw materials for new pharmaceuticals to treat disease.

The anti-cancer agents taxol and vinblastine are derived from the Pacific yew and rosy periwinkle (Figure 10.1), respectively. Analgesics come from plants: morphine from the sap of poppies and salicylic acid (the main component of aspirin) from the bark of willows. Medical researchers are currently surveying numerous plants, many from the tropics, for new chemical compounds.

Plants also perform essential ecosystem services. Through their productivity, plants provide the energy that a vast majority of all life depends on to survive. The hydrologic cycle, climatic patterns, oxygen production, nutrient turnover, and all other processes vital to ecosystem function are regulated by plants. And these essential life-sustaining services (estimated to have an economic value of over $33 trillion[6]) are provided at no cost.

Finally, plant diversity is important for its aesthetic and cultural value. Natural landscapes and the organisms they contain are things of great beauty. In his classic book, *A Sand County Almanac*, naturalist and philosopher Aldo Leopold wrote extensively of the importance of nature for not only sustaining human life but also human culture. More recently, prominent conservation biologists such as E. O. Wilson have argued that because of its importance in sustaining life, conservation of nature is a moral issue.

THE IMPORTANCE OF SPECIES ABUNDANCE

The goal of conservation is to prevent species from becoming **extinct**. Conservation biologists classify species based upon their probability of going extinct. A **threatened species** is one whose populations are showing a decline in numbers in part or all of its range. **Endangered species,** such as the Pecos sunflower, Penland's beardtongue, or the western prairie fringed orchid are ones whose populations have declined to such low numbers that extinction is likely throughout all or part of its range. Within the United States, 584 angiosperm species, 3 gymnosperm species, 26 ferns and fern allies, and 2 lichen species are currently listed as threatened or endangered (see "Seaside Alder" box, Figure 10.2).

Species at the greatest risk of extinction have either narrow ecological tolerances or limited geographic range. Many of these species are **endemics**, which occur in a particular location such as an island or a single mountain range. For example, many of the endangered plants in the United States are endemic to the Hawaiian Islands. Although Hawaii has only 0.2% of the U.S. land area, it is home to 44% of the threatened and endangered plants.[7] The inherently low frequency of occurrence makes endemic species particularly vulnerable to extinction.

Extinction itself is a natural process and many species have evolved and died out over Earth's history. There have been five major extinction events over the past 600,000,000 years of life on Earth (Table 10.1). Climate change caused the first four and the fifth (the one that killed the dinosaurs) was likely caused by meteorite strikes and volcanic activity. However, the current extinction crisis is being driven primarily by human activities, which gives cause for tremendous concern.

Seaside Alder

Seaside alder is one of the rarest tree species in the world (Figure 10.2). While most North American alders are widely distributed, seaside alder grows in only three locations: the Delmarva Peninsula of Delaware and Maryland, south-central Oklahoma, and northwestern Georgia. These isolated populations are relics of what was once a more extensive and continuous distribution since the last glaciation of North America. Seaside alder can grow only in areas that are adjacent to or in moving water and have exposure to full sun. Although trees produce numerous, viable seeds, there is no evidence of seedling establishment in any of the populations. This indicates that environmental conditions necessary for seaside alder establishment no longer exist. At present, the remaining adult trees are able to survive along the edges of waterways where they grow. However, if there is any change in water availability in these areas due to increased use of water by humans or other factors, the remaining seaside alders will probably not be able to survive, and this species may become extinct.

Figure 10.2 Seaside alder is one of the rarest tree species in the world. It was once widely distributed across North America, but today it grows only in the Delmarva Peninsula in Delaware and Maryland, Oklahoma, and Georgia.

HABITAT DESTRUCTION

Destruction and alteration of natural habitats is the leading cause of extinctions. At present, tropical deforestation is the greatest threat to biodiversity. Over 0.6% of tropical forest is cleared each year. However, other biomes have been subject to extensive damage in the past. Temperate forests have been cut, prairies have been plowed, and wetlands have been drained.

Habitats are damaged as a result of the expanding human population and its need for space. It is estimated that 39%–50% of Earth's terrestrial environments have been transformed by human activity.[8] Vegetation is cleared to make room for agriculture and for expanding cities. Valleys are flooded in efforts to control and manage water resources. As a consequence, water diverted for human use is not available to support ecosystems. Humans alone monopolize over 50% of all freshwater resources.[9]

INVASIVE SPECIES

As humans have traveled around the planet, they have taken plant species with them. Whether the plants were intentionally carried to new areas as foodstuffs, ornamentals, or medicines, or unintentionally transported in cargo, species have been introduced into new areas far removed from where they initially evolved. Some of these transported species are not capable of escaping the confines of the field or garden, and therefore have had little impact on the **native species**. Other species, unfortunately, perform all too well in their new environment and

Table 10.1 Mass Extinctions in Earth's History

GEOLOGIC PERIOD	MILLIONS OF YEARS AGO
Quarternary	Present
Cretaceous	65
Triassic	213
Permian	248
Devonian	360
Ordovician	438

escape into the wild to grow and reproduce. When this occurs, they are referred to as **invasive species** (see "Kudzu and Purple Loosestrife" box, Figure 10.3).

When invasive species are introduced into a new area, they often experience unchecked population growth because of ecological differences between their old habitat and the new one. The climate in the new area can be different from where they originated, which can allow for extended growing seasons. Plants introduced into a new area may also be freed from herbivores, parasites, or competitors that keep their populations in check in their native environment.

Species introductions can have a cascade of detrimental effects on communities. For example, once invasive species begin to dominate a community, native species are replaced. When native plants are gone, organisms that depend on them are without critical elements of their habitat, causing them to go locally extinct as well. These changes in community composition continue to affect other species in the community.

Kudzu and Purple Loosestrife

Two of the most devastating species introduced into North America are kudzu and purple loosestrife. Kudzu was introduced to the United States from Japan in the 1930s to be used for erosion control. Warm conditions in the southeast promote rapid, prolific growth of this species. Vines can grow at a rate of 5 cm (2 inches) per hour during peak conditions. Vines engulf and kill trees, cover hillsides, and choke out native vegetation. Purple loosestrife was introduced as an ornamental and accidentally in ships' ballast. One plant can set over 2 million seeds per year. Purple loosestrife is an aggressive competitor that rapidly dominates and replaces native wetland species. Though the plants do have their uses, they have devastated many plant communities and cost millions of dollars worth of damage.

Figure 10.3 Purple loosestrife is an invasive species that is an aggressive competitor that quickly dominates native plant species.

Many prairies have been severely impacted by introduced grasses that out-compete the native species for water and other resources, and consequently replace them. For example, cheat grass, Japanese brome, and barnyard grass have established in grasslands throughout North America. Many native plants of California have been threatened by species introduced from around the world that were seeds in grains unloaded in Pacific ports. Islands are particularly susceptible to species introductions. There are 1,200 native plant species on Hawaii (90% of them endemic), but the 4,600 plant species introduced by humans are replacing the native flora.

Introduced plants are not the only problems. Introduced animals, fungi, and bacteria also threaten plant species with extinction. Like many island species, endemic palms that evolved in Hawaii have lost the defense mechanisms present in their ancestors that originally colonized the islands. Because they have lost these defenses, they are being driven to extinction by pigs (introduced by Polynesian and European colonists) that eat young palm saplings and the roots of mature trees. Epidemic outbreaks of introduced insects such as the hemlock wooly adelgid are currently devastating hemlock forests throughout the Atlantic states.

One of the worst cases of an introduced species pushing a species to the brink of extinction is chestnut blight, which was accidentally introduced into the United States on nursery plants from China in 1900. This disease spread rapidly and killed almost all of the chestnut trees in eastern North America. Those that cling to life sprout suckers from their roots that grow for a brief period of time before succumbing to the disease. Chestnut was a dominant forest species whose loss has dramatically altered the ecology of eastern hardwood forests. Sudden oak death is a disease that is currently being monitored to prevent similar devastation of North American forests.

POLLUTION

Pollution can take many forms. The Everglades ecosystem of southern Florida, for example, has been by polluted with fertilizer runoff from sugarcane fields. The Everglades is a 4,500-square-mile marsh ecosystem in the Kissimee River drainage. Increased nutrient levels (primarily phosphorus) in the water have stimulated the growth of cattails, which are replacing native species such as sawgrass. Over 30,000 acres of this unique ecosystem have already been damaged due to water pollution. Although steps have been taken to reduce phosphorus levels in water, cattails are continuing to spread at a rate of two acres per day.

Atmospheric pollution presents another ecological threat to plants. The two greatest concerns are acid rain and greenhouse gases. All precipitation is somewhat acidic (average pH = 5.6) due to atmospheric carbon dioxide (CO_2) mixing with water vapor to form carbonic acid. Acid rain is any rain, snow, or fog that has a pH less than 5.6. Acid rain forms when sulfur dioxide (SO_2) and nitrogen oxides (NO_x), released by the burning of fossil fuels, react with water vapor in clouds leading to the formation of sulfuric and nitric acids.

Acid rain impacts vegetation in several ways (Figure 10.4). It damages the waxy **cuticle** layer on the leaf surface. Once the cuticle is damaged, plants are more susceptible to disease, insect attack, and nutrient loss. Vital soil processes are also altered. Acid rain decreases soil pH, which allows more nutrients to leach out of the soil. It also increases the availability of metals such as lead that are toxic to plants. Increased soil acidity also kills mutualistic mycorrhizal fungi that are important for plant nutrient uptake.

Another serious pollution problem is global climate change. This problem is often described as the "greenhouse effect." However, the greenhouse effect itself is actually a vital process. Gasses in the atmosphere trap heat, which keeps the planet warm enough to sustain life. The real problem is the increase of atmospheric greenhouse gases, which is causing more heat to be retained (Figure 10.5). The primary greenhouse gas of concern is CO_2 released by the burning of fossil fuels.

It is not just the increased temperature that is of concern but the shifts in current climate patterns caused by warming. Middle- and high-latitude regions will become warmer. Some

Figure 10.4 Atmospheric pollution (particularly from the burning of fossil fuels) often returns to Earth in the form of acid rain, which has a devastating effect on trees and other vegetation. Acid rain changes the soil pH, increases heavy metals, and damages the cuticle layer of leaves.

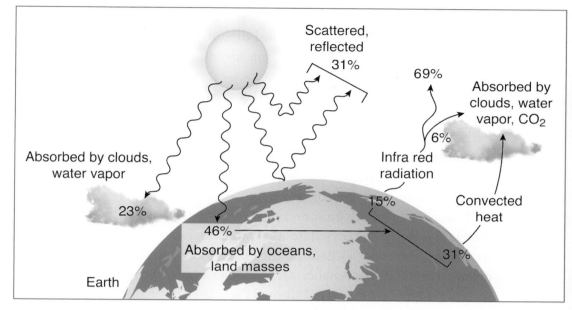

Figure 10.5 An increase in atmospheric greenhouse gases, particularly carbon dioxide, cause more heat to be retained, a phenomenon known as global warming. Global warming could potentially shift current climate patterns, affecting plant biomes and species distribution.

areas will receive more rain while others will become drier. In response to these climatic changes, biome and species distributions will shift. For example, with warmer temperatures, the geographic range of temperate species such as sugar maple and beech will shift northward where the cooler temperatures they require can be found. If these and other plants are unable to disperse their seeds into new areas in response to climate change, they will face extinction.

PROTECTING HABITATS AND SPECIES

Many of these ecological problems can be addressed through legislation. The Endangered Species Act of 1973 has successfully provided federal protection to species that face the threat of extinction. Likewise, legislation has been effectively used to prevent some forms of pollution that threaten species and communities. Further legislative and diplomatic efforts, based on sound scientific data, are urgently needed to address and solve these problems.

Another way to protect species and ecosystems is through the development and management of conservation areas such as parks and preserves (Figure 10.6). The remaining natural areas have been isolated into islands in a sea of human development. These habitat fragments must be protected and managed if they are to continue to protect biodiversity.

The use of conservation areas is based upon **Island Biogeographic Theory.** This theory states that larger areas are capable of sustaining more species because they have more resources and diverse habitats than smaller areas. For example, more plant species are typically found in National Parks than in smaller state parks (see "Protected Land in the U.S." box,). Smaller parks, however, are not without value—conservation biologists have

Protected Land in the U.S.

In 1908, President Theodore Roosevelt and the head of the U.S. Forest Service, Gifford Pinchot, began developing a system of national forests and reserves to protect the natural resources of the United States. John Muir, the first president of the Sierra Club, also spoke out for preservation and protection, not only for its resource value but also for its own sake. The work of these men led to the establishment of the National Park Service in 1916. Currently, over 645 million acres are federally protected or managed by the National Park Service, U.S. Fish and Wildlife Service, and U.S. Forest Service. Many more areas are protected by states and private conservation groups such as the Nature Conservancy. Worldwide, it is estimated that over 3,000 protected areas have been established that protect over 1 billion acres.

Figure 10.6 One way to protect plant species and fragile ecosystems is through the development of conservation areas such as national parks, forests, and preserves.

shown that establishing a large protected area that is connected with several smaller protected areas is an effective strategy for preserving species.

Summary

Human activities are adversely affecting the biodiversity of Earth. As with all organisms, plants are threatened by loss of habitat, environmental pollution, invasive species, and other impacts due to the growth of the human population. Acid rain and global climate change are major changes in the environment that are impacting many plant species. Through implementing a variety of conservation strategies, many habitats and species can be protected and preserved.

Appendix

Common and Scientific Names for Plant Species

The notation spp. is used to indicate all members of a genus.

Common Name	Scientific Name
acacia	*Acacia* spp.
agave	*Agave* spp.
alder	*Alnus* spp.
alfalfa	*Medicago sativa*
alpine pennycress	*Thlaspi caerulescens*
amaranth	*Amaranthus* spp.
American chestnut	*Castanea dentata*
aguacatillo	*Ocotea tenera*
avocado	*Persea americana*
azalea	*Rohododendron*
bald cypress	*Taxodium distichum*
bamboo	*Bambusa* spp.
banana	*Musa* spp.
barley	*Hordeum vulgare*
barnyard grass	*Echinoichloa crus-gali*
bean	*Phaseolus vulgaris*
beech	*Fagus grandifolia*
beggar's lice	*Hackelia virginiana*
big bluestem	*Andropogon gerardii*
birch	*Betula* spp.
blue spruce	*Picea pungens*
broomsedge	*Andropogon virginicus*
cannabis	*Cannabis sativa*
cardinal flower	*Lobelia cardinalis*
carrion flower	*Stapelia gigantea*
cassava	*Manihot esculenta*
cattail	*Typha latifolia*

ceanothus	*Ceanothus* spp.
cedar, eastern red	*Juniperus virginiana*
century plant	*Agave* spp.
chamise	*Adenostoma* spp.
cheat grass	*Bromus tectorum*
chestnut	*Castanea* spp.
chick peas	*Cicer arietinum*
clover	*Trifolium repens*
club moss	*Lycopodium* spp.
coast redwood	*Sequoia sempervierens*
cocklebur	*Xanthium strumarium*
coconut palm	*Cocos* spp.
coffee	*Coffea arabica*
columbine, Sierra	*Aquilegia pubescens*
columbine, western	*Aquilegia formosa*
compass plant	*Silphium laciniatum*
corn	*Zea mays*
cotton	*Gossypium* spp.
cottonwood	*Populus deltoides*
crabgrass	*Digitaria sanguinalis*
curly cup gumweed	*Grindelia ciliata*
dandelion	*Taraxacum officinale*
datura	*Datura stramonium*
dead nettle	*Lamium* spp.
devil's walking stick	*Fouquiera splendens*
dodder	*Cuscutta* spp.
dogbane	*Apocynum* spp.
dogwood	*Cornus florida*
Douglas fir	*Pseudotsuga menziesii*
drakea orchid	*Drakea* spp.
dwarf mistletoe	*Arceuthobium vaginatum*
eucalyptus	*Eucalyptus* spp.

field bean	*Vicia faba*
fir	*Abies* spp.
fir, subalpine	*Abies lasiocarpa*
foxglove	*Digitalis purpurea*
giant sequoia	*Sequoiadendron giganteum*
ginkgo	*Ginkgo biloba*
hemlock	*Tsuga* spp.
hickory	*Carya* spp.
holly	*Ilex* spp.
horsetail	*Equisetum* spp.
horseweed	*Conyza canadensis*
Indian grass	*Sorghastrum nutans*
Indian pipe	*Monotropa uniflora*
iris	*Iris* spp.
ironweed	*Vernonia baldwinii*
Japanese brome	*Bromus japonicus*
juniper	*Juniperus* spp.
kudzu	*Pueraria montana*
larch	*Larix* spp.
lentils	*Lens culinaris*
little bluestem	*Schizachyrium scoparium*
liverwort	*Marchantia* spp.
lobelia	*Lobelia* spp.
magnolia	*Magnolia* spp.
maple	*Acer* spp.
maple, mountain	*Acer glabrum*
maple, red	*Acer rubrum*
marigold	*Tagetes* spp.
maypop	*Berberis* spp.
milkweed	*Asclepias* spp.
millet	*Pennisetum glaucum*
mistletoe	*Phoradendron serotinum*

mountain laurel	*Kalmia latifolia*
needle grass	*Achnatherum* spp.
oak	*Quercus* spp.
oak, chestnut	*Quercus prinus*
oak, Georgia	*Quercus georgiana*
oak, post	*Quercus stellata*
oak, scrub	*Quercus berberidifolia*
oak, white	*Quercus alba*
oats	*Avena sativa*
oleander	*Nerium oleander*
Pacific yew	*Taxus brevifolia*
pea	*Pisum* spp.
peanut	*Arachis hypogea*
Pecos sunflower	*Helianthus paradoxus*
Penland's beardtongue	*Pentstemmon penlandii*
peyote	*Lophophora williamsii*
phlox	*Galium* spp.
pigeon pea	*Cajanus cajan*
pine	*Pinus* spp.
pine, bristlecone	*Pinus longaeva*
pine, loblolly	*Pinus taeda*
pine, lodgepole	*Pinus contorta*
pine, longleaf	*Pinus palustris*
pine, pitch	*Pinus rigida*
pine, ponderosa	*Pinus ponderosa*
pine, shortleaf	*Pinus echinata*
pine, table mountain	*Pinus pungens*
pine, whitebark	*Pinus albicaulis*
pineapple	*Ananas comosus*
pitcher plant	*Sarracenia* spp.
poison hemlock	*Conium maculatum*
pool sprite	*Amphianthus pusillus*

poppy	*Papaver* spp.
poppy, Oriental	*Papaver somniferum*
potato	*Solanum tuberosum*
prickly pear	*Opuntia* spp.
purple loosestrife	*Lythrum salicaria*
quaking aspen	*Populus tremuloides*
ragweed	*Ambrosia* spp.
reindeer moss	*Cladonia* spp.
rhododendron	*Rhododendron* spp.
rice, Africa	*Oryza glaberrima*
rice, Asian	*Oryza sativa*
rose	*Rosa* spp.
rosy periwinkle	*Cathranthus roseus*
rye	*Secale cereale*
sacred lotus	*Nelumbo nucifera*
sagebrush	*Artemesia* spp.
sawgrass	*Cladium mariscus*
seaside alder	*Alnus maritima*
sorghum	*Sorghum bicolor*
sourwood	*Oxydendrum arboreum*
soybean	*Glycine max*
Spanish needles	*Bidens pilosa*
sparkleberry	*Vaccinium arboreum*
spruce	*Picea* spp.
squash	*Cucurbita* spp.
sticky cinquefoil	*Potentilla glandulosa*
stinging nettle	*Urtica dioica*
stonecrop	*Diamorpha smallii*
strangler fig	*Ficus* spp.
strawberry	*Frageria* spp.
sugar beet	*Beta vulgaris*
sugarcane	*Saccharum officinarum*

sundew	*Drosera* spp.
sunflower	*Helianthus annuus*
sweet potato	*Ipomoea batatas*
switch grass	*Panicum virgatum*
thistle	*Cirsium* spp.
tobacco	*Nicotiana tabacum*
tomato	*Lycopersicon esculentum*
tulip	*Tulipa* spp.
tumbleweed	*Salsola kali*
tussock grass	*Nassella* spp.
Venus flytrap	*Dionaea muscipula*
vetch	*Astragalus* spp.
walnut, black	*Juglans nigra*
water celery	*Vallisneria americana*
western prairie fringed orchid	*Platanthera praeclara*
wheat	*Triticum aestivum*
whisk fern	*Psilotum* spp.
white aster	*Aster* spp.
wild rice	*Zizania latifolia*
willow	*Salix* spp.
wood sorrel	*Oxalis* spp.
yarrow	*Achillea millefolium*
yucca	*Yucca* spp.
ophrys orchid	*Ophrys* spp.

Glossary

Abiotic Nonliving.

Acclimation Physiological adjustment of an organism in response to an environmental factor such as temperature or light levels.

Achene A dry single-seeded fruit such as a sunflower seed.

Adaptations Genetically determined characteristics that allow organisms to survive and reproduce in a particular environment.

Agronomist A scientist who studies agricultural crops.

Allelopathy Chemical inhibition of one plant by another.

Alpine tundra Cold grassland biome restricted to mountaintops above treeline.

Anemochory Seed dispersal by wind.

Angiosperm A plant that produces flowers and whose seeds are contained within a fruit.

Annual A plant that completes its life cycle in one year.

Anther Floral structure in which pollen is produced.

Arctic tundra Cold grassland biome restricted to polar regions.

Artificial selection The selective breeding of crops or livestock to increase the occurrence of desirable traits.

Beltian bodies Protein-rich structures found on acacia leaves that ants feed to their larvae.

Biodiversity The different types of organisms within an ecosystem.

Biogeography The study of geographic distributions of organisms.

Biomass The mass of all the living organisms in an area.

Biomes Large geographic regions of terrestrial habitat that support similar ecosystems.

Biotic Living.

Bract A modified leaf-like structure that can be part of a flower or fruit.

Browsers Animals that eat leaves and other tissues from woody plants.

Bryophytes A group of non-flowering plants including mosses, liverworts, hornworts, and quillworts.

Bulb A fleshy underground structure found in herbaceous perennials such as lilies.

C_3 photosynthesis Photosynthetic pathway used by most plants in which CO_2 is initially assimilated to form a 3-carbon compound as the first stable molecule.

C_4 photosynthesis Modified photosynthetic system commonly used by plants in arid, high light environments in which CO_2 is assimilated into a 4-carbon compound as the first stable molecule and then transported to the bundle sheath, where the CO_2 is released and fixed via the C_3 pathway.

(CAM) photosynthesis See Crassulacean Acid Metabolism (CAM) photosynthesis.

Canopy The tallest layer of trees in a forest.

Capsule A dry fruit type that opens along multiple seams to release seeds.

Carbon fixation Process in which a photosynthetic enzyme takes up CO_2 inside a leaf to begin photosynthesis.

Carrying capacity The maximum size of a population that can survive in an area.

Chaparral A scrub forest biome found in semi-arid coastal regions with hot, dry summers and cool, mild winters.

Chlorophyll Group of green pigments responsible for capturing much of the light used in photosynthesis.

Chloroplast The structure within plant cells that contains the enzymes and pigments necessary for photosynthesis.

Glossary

Climate The long-term pattern of precipitation and temperature for an area.

Climax community A stable, self-sustaining community that occurs at the end of succession.

Clone A group of genetically identical individuals.

Coevolution The close interaction of species that leads each to undergo adaptations that enhance their interdependency.

Commensalism Interaction in which one organism benefits while the other is unaffected.

Community A group of populations of different species co-existing and interacting with one another.

Competition Interaction that harms both species when they exist together.

Cone A compact collection of reproductive structures on scales attached to a short axis that produces either pollen or seeds, typically found in gymnosperms and other groups of non-flowering plants.

Consumers Organisms that obtain energy and nutrients from other organisms.

Corm A dry underground structure found in perennial plants such as gladiolus.

Crassulacean Acid Metabolism (CAM) photosynthesis Photosynthetic system that allows plants in extremely hot, dry environments to take up CO_2 at night, minimizing water loss.

Crop rotation The process of increasing nutrients levels in the soil by planting nitrogen-fixing cover crops in alternation with a cash crop.

Crown fires Fires that burn extremely hot and spread from treetop to treetop.

Cuticle Waxy, protective layer on the outer surfaces of leaves.

Deciduous Plant that loses its leaves during autumn or the dry season.

Decomposers Organisms that break down leaf litter, animal wastes, and dead animals.

Desert An extremely dry biome that also has extreme heat or cold; typically supports little vegetation.

Dioecy A plant reproductive system in which male and female flowers are produced on different plants.

Disturbance Any force or phenomenon in the environment that disrupts the standing vegetation.

Diversity A measure of the numbers and relative proportions of different species in a community.

Dominant One or more species that make up the majority of individuals in a community.

Drought deciduous Plants that shed their leaves as conditions become more dry.

Ecology The study of the interactions between organisms and their environment.

Ecosystem A functioning system of organisms interacting with the environment.

Ecotone A transitional area between adjacent, contrasting plant communities.

Ecotype A population adapted to the local environmental conditions.

Ectozoochory Seed dispersal that involves a seed attaching to the outside of an animal.

Elaiosome A small structure rich in lipids and sterols attached to some seeds.

Emergents Trees which extend above the forest canopy.

Endangered species A species that has a high probability of becoming extinct.

Glossary

Endemic A species that occurs in only a specific location in specific environmental conditions.

Endozoochory Seed dispersal that involves a seed being consumed by an animal.

Environment The external conditions that affect an organism during its lifetime.

Epiphytes Non-parasitic plants that grow on trees.

Erosion Processes by which wind or water loosens soil in one area and deposits it in another.

Evenness The relative numbers of individuals in a species in a community.

Evergreen Tree whose leaves can be shed at any time of year, but never all at once.

Evolution A change in genetically based characteristics of a species over time.

Extinct A species which has ceased to exist either in a particular region or globally.

Ferns and fern allies Group of plants including ferns, horsetails, and club mosses that have vascular tissue but reproduce by spores.

Fertilization The joining of egg and sperm in sexual reproduction.

Floret A small flower.

Flower Reproductive structure of angiosperms composed of sepals, petals, stamens, and carpels.

Food chain A series of organisms that pass energy from one trophic level to the next.

Frugivores Animals that eat fruits.

Fungi Kingdom of organisms that have cell walls and obtain their food through absorption.

Genetically modified organism (GMO) Organism whose genetic makeup has been modified through genetic engineering.

Genotype The genetic sequence or sequences in the DNA that "code" for a given trait.

Germination The resumption of growth by a dormant spore, seed, or pollen grain.

Granivores Animals that eat seeds.

Grasslands Biome type dominated by grasses in semi-arid areas with hot summers and cold winters.

Grazers Animals that eat mostly grasses.

Growth rings Pattern of rings formed in the wood of temperate trees and shrubs; each ring is equal to one year of growth.

Gross primary productivity (GPP) The total amount of energy converted by plants from sunlight.

Gymnosperm A plant that reproduces using cones and bears exposed "naked" seeds (i.e., not contained in fruits).

Gynodioecy A plant reproductive system in which some plants produce hermaphroditic flowers and other plants produce female flowers.

Habitat The location where an organism lives.

Hemiparasite A parasite that receives only part of the resources it requires to live from its host.

Herbaceous Non-woody plant tissue.

Herbivory Interaction in which animals eat plants.

Herbivores Animals that eat plants.

Hermaphroditic Flowers that contain both male and female structures.

Heterocarpy The production of two or more distinct types of fruits by different flowers on the same plant.

Glossary

Hydrochory Water-aided seed dispersal.

Inflorescence A cluster of flowers close to one another on a stem.

Integrated pest management Pest control approach that uses biological and ecological approaches to controlling pest populations in addition to minor use of chemical pesticides.

Invasive species A species that is introduced into a new area where it replaces the native species.

Island Biogeographic Theory A theory that predicts larger areas will be able to sustain more species than smaller areas.

Iteroparous Organisms that produce offspring many times over the life of the individual.

K-strategists Organisms whose life history traits promote survival of the individual in stable populations at or near the carrying capacity, typically with a large investment of resources in individual offspring.

Krumholtz A growth form meaning "twisted wood" applied to normally tall, straight trees that grow as low, twisted shrubs because of environmental conditions at the treeline.

Lapse rate The change in temperature that occurs as latitude or elevation changes.

Leaf litter The layer of dead leaves and branches on the forest floor.

Liana A woody vine.

Life history The life cycle and reproductive characteristics of a species that influence survival and the production of offspring.

Lichens Organisms that result from a symbiotic relationship between a fungus and an algae.

Meristem Localized region of cell division and growth in plants.

Mesophyll The middle layer of a leaf.

Microclimate Environmental conditions in a localized area.

Mimicry Ecological strategy in which one species resembles another species or some other component of the environment.

Monoculture The cultivation of large tracts of land with a single crop.

Monoecy Reproductive system in which a separate male and female flowers are produced on the same plant.

Montane coniferous forest See Taiga.

Mutualism An interaction that benefits both participating species.

Mycorrhizae Fungi that associate with plant roots.

Native species A species in its original range.

Natural selection A process of evolutionary change that occurs when genetic change produces individuals with greater reproductive success or greater survival.

Nectar A sweet secretion produced by plants for the purpose of attracting animals, often produced in flowers to attract pollinators.

Nectar robbers Insects that steal nectar without providing any pollination service.

Net primary productivity (NPP) The amount of energy produced through photosynthesis remaining after plants meet their own energetic needs.

Niche An organism's job in the community, reflecting the way it gathers and uses resources and interacts with other organisms.

No tillage Method of planting seeds with little or no disturbance of the soil.

Old growth forest A community comprised of trees that have greatly surpassed the typical life span for the species.

Old-field succession Secondary succession in an abandoned agricultural field.

Ovary The enlarged, seed-producing portion of a flower that, after fertilization, becomes a fruit.

Glossary

Pappus Hooks, barbs, or feather-like structures on the top of achenes in the sunflower family.

Parasitism An interaction in which one organism obtains its food and nutrients from a host organism; typically the host is harmed but the parasite benefits.

Perennial A plant that lives for more than two years and typically reproduces repeatedly throughout its life.

Permafrost The perpetually frozen layer beneath the soil surface in the tundra.

Pesticides A chemical substance used to eradicate harmful insects, fungi, or weeds.

Petal The part of a flower that is often brightly colored.

Phenotype Any characteristic (structural, biochemical, or behavioral) expressed by an organism.

Phenotypic plasticity The shaping of an organism's characteristic traits by the environmental conditions in which it lives.

Photoperiod A combination of light and dark periods, often indicative of seasonal change, that stimulates a plant response.

Photorespiration A process by which plants consume sugar and release CO_2.

Photosynthesis The process through which plants convert the energy in light into sugars and oxygen using water and CO_2.

Plant ecology The study of the relationship between plants and their environment.

Pollen A structure containing the sperm cells in angiosperms and gymnosperms.

Pollen tube A tube that develops from a pollen grain and carries the sperm to the egg.

Pollination In angiosperms, the transfer of pollen from an anther to a stigma; in gymnosperms, the transfer of pollen from a male cone to a female cone.

Pollination droplet A sticky secretion that catches pollen outside a gymnosperm cone and brings it into the cone for fertilization.

Population All the individuals of the same species living in the same area at the same time.

Prairies A temperate grassland biome.

Preformation The production of flower buds several years in advance of their blooming; common in the tundra.

Primary productivity The energy converted from sunlight into sugars through photosynthesis.

Primary succession A series of changes in a plant community that occurs on bare substrates that have not supported vegetation in the past.

Producers Organisms such as plants and algae that convert the energy in sunlight into organic molecules; producers form the foundation of a food chain in an ecosystem.

Pseudocopulation An attempt by an insect to mate with a flower that resembles an insect, resulting in pollen being transferred from one flower to another.

r-strategists Organisms whose traits promote rapid maturation and the production of many offspring; typically there is little resource investment by the parent in each individual offspring.

Rain forest Biome that receives high quantities of precipitation throughout the year, common in tropical regions.

Range A geographic area in which populations of a species occur.

Reduced tillage Method of readying soil for planting that disturbs soil less than tillage.

Respiration Metabolic process in which sugars and oxygen are combined resulting in CO_2, water, and energy.

Rhizome Fleshy, horizontal underground stem.

Richness The number of different species in a community.

Glossary

Riparian Zone along a creek or river.

Root apical meristem Regions of cell division and growth at the tip of roots.

Ruderals Annuals that live in areas in which the vegetation is disturbed, but there are ample resources available.

Runners A stem that grows along the ground and produces plants through vegetative reproduction.

Safe sites Locations that are suitable for the germination and establishment of new plants.

Samara Fruit type in which a wing is attached to an achene and aids in wind dispersal of seeds; typical in maples.

Savanna Tropical grassland biome dominated by grasses and scattered trees.

Secondary succession A series of changes that occurs in a community where the vegetation has been disturbed, but the soil remains.

Sedge A grasslike plant that is commonly found in wet or cold environments.

Seed A structure consisting a dormant plant embryo and its nutritional reserves surrounded by a seed coat.

Seed coat Layer of tissue surrounding a seed, may be thin or hardened in different species.

Scarification The physical or chemical weakening of the seed coat that enables the seed to germinate.

Self-thinning A process in which competition causes individuals in a population to die and population density is, consequently, decreased.

Semelparous Organisms that produce offspring once during their lifetime and then die.

Sepal Leaf-like outermost structure of a flower.

Seral stages Different communities that occur over the course of ecological succession.

Sere The sequence of changes in a community undergoing succession.

Serotiny A reproductive strategy used by some pines in which cones remain closed until opened by fire to release the seeds inside.

Sexual reproduction The formation of offspring by combining sperm and eggs.

Shoot apical meristem Regions of cell division and growth at the tip of stems.

Species A particular type of organism that can be differentiated from other types of organisms; all members of a species have the ability to interbreed and they share a common evolutionary history.

Spores Single-celled reproductive structures in bryophytes, ferns, and fern allies that are capable of developing into plants.

Spur Modified petal or sepal that has a tubular shape and contains nectar.

Stamen "Male" part of the flower that produces pollen, composed of anther and filament.

Stigma The receptive portion of the carpel upon which pollen grains germinate.

Stolons A long branch that grows along the ground and produces plants through vegetative reproduction.

Stomata Openings in the leaf surface that allow a plant to take in CO_2 and release O_2.

Stratification The exposure of seed to moisture followed by a period of cold temperatures.

Style The carpel tissue that connects the stigma to the ovary; pollen tubes grow through the style to reach the ovary.

Succession A series of predictable, cumulative changes in the composition and characteristics of a plant community following disturbance.

Glossary

Succulent A fleshy stem or leaf that stores a high quantity of water.

Surface fires Fires that occur above ground and are not extremely hot.

Sustainable agriculture Agricultural methods that do not harm the environment and can, therefore, be maintained for long periods of time.

Symbiotic Relationship in which both individuals benefit from the interaction and are harmed when they are not together.

Taiga A forest biome type in cold areas that is dominated by one or few species, primarily pines, spruces, and firs.

Temperate coniferous forest A forest biome type in temperate regions dominated by pines and other gymnosperms.

Temperate deciduous forest A forest biome type in temperate regions with high rainfall and strong seasonal differences; most trees drop their leaves in the fall and are dormant during the winter.

Temperate grasslands See Prairie.

Tepal A sepal that has the color or shape of a petal.

Threatened species A species that is experiencing a decline in population size and numbers.

Tillage The process of working soil to make it suitable for growing crops.

Treeline The elevation above which environmental conditions are too extreme for trees to grow.

Tropical dry forest Forest biome type in tropical regions that experiences a dry season in which many trees drop their leaves.

Tropical rain forest Forest biome type in tropical regions which receives high amounts of rain and has a year-round growing season; has the highest species diversity of any biome type.

Tuber Fleshy, underground stem used for storage in perennial species such as potato.

Understory The layer of smaller trees and other plants below the forest canopy.

Vascular cambium Meristem sandwiched between the xylem and phloem that produces new vascular tissue and contributes to increased diameter of woody stems.

Vascular tissue Tissue in plants used for transporting of water and minerals around the plant body.

Vegetative (or asexual) reproduction Reproduction that uses growth from existing stems or roots to produce a new plant rather than combining sperm and egg.

Weed Opportunistic species that grow predominantly in disturbed areas.

Wood Secondary xylem produced by the vascular cambium.

Zoochory Seed dispersal by animals.

Notes

1. *National Interagency Fire Center Wildland Fire Statistics.* Available online at http://www.nifc.gov/stats/wildlandfirestats.html.

2. P.M. Vitousek, H.A. Mooney, J. Lubchenco, and J.M. Melillo, "Human Domination of Earth's Ecosystems," *Science* 277 (1997): 494–499.

3. S.D. Schubert, M.J. Suarez, P.J. Pegion, R.D. Koster, and J.T. Bacmeister, "On the Cause of the 1930s Dust Bowl," *Science* 303 (2004): 1855–1859.

4. F. Osborn, *Our Plundered Planet.* Boston: Little, Brown, 1948, p. 201.

5. E.O. Wilson, *The Future of Life.* New York: Vintage Books, 2002, p. 119.

6. *U.S. Fish and Wildlife Service Threatened and Endangered Species System.* Available online at http://ecos.fws.gov/tess_public/TESSBoxscore.

7. M.C. Mollis, *Ecology Concepts and Applications.* New York: McGraw-Hill, 2002, p. 444.

8. P.M. Vitousek, H.A. Mooney, J. Lubchenco, and J.M. Melillo, "Human Domination of Earth's Ecosystems," *Science* 277 (1997): 494–499.

9. D. Hinrichsen, "A Human Thirst," in *Annual Editions: Environment 2004/2005.* Dubuque, IA: McGraw-Hill/Dushkin, 2004, p. 173.

Books and Journals

Abrams, M. D. "The Red Maple Paradox." *BioScience* 48 (1998): 355–364.

Anderson, E. *Plants, Man and Life.* St. Louis, MO: Missouri Botanical Garden, 1997.

Antonovics, J. A., A. N. Bradshaw, and R. G. Turner. "Heavy Metal Tolerance in Plants." *Annual Review of Ecology and Systematics* 71 (1971): 1–85.

Barbour, M. G., J. H. Burk, and W. D. Pitts. *Terrestrial Plant Ecology.* Menlo Park, CA: Benjamin/Cummings, 1987.

Baskin, C. C., and J. M. Baskin. *Seeds. Ecology, Biogeography, and Evolution of Dormancy and Germination.* San Diego, CA: Academic Press, 1998.

Bawa, K. S. "Evolution of Dioecy in Flowering Plants." *Annual Review of Ecology and Systematics* 11 (1980): 15–39.

Bawa, K. S., and J. H. Beach. "Evolution of Sexual Systems in Flowering Plants." *Annals of the Missouri Botanical Garden* 68 (1981): 254–274.

Brown, K. S. "Life on the Molecular Farm." *BioScience* 46 (1996): 80–83.

Burbanck, M. P., and R. B. Platt. "Granite Outcrop Communities of the Piedmont Plateau in Georgia." *Ecology* 45 (1964): 292–305.

Enger, E. D., and B. F. Smith. *Environmental Science: A Study of Interrelationships,* 10th ed. New York: McGraw-Hill, 2004.

Futuyma, D. J. *Evolution.* Sunderland, MA: Sinauer, 2005.

Gibson, J. P. "Ecological and Genetic Comparison Between Ray and Disc Achene Pools of the Heteromorphic Species *Prionopsis ciliata* (Asteraceae)." *International Journal of Plant Sciences* 162 (2001): 137–145

Gibson, J. P., and J. L. Hamrick. "Genetic Diversity and Structure in *Pinus pungens* (Table Mountain Pine) Populations." *Canadian Journal of Forest Research* 21 (1991): 635–642.

Gibson, J. P., and A. J. Pollard. "Zinc Tolerance in *Panicum virgatum* L. (Switchgrass) From the Picher Mine Area." *Proceedings of the Oklahoma Academy of Sciences* 68 (1988): 45–49.

Bibliography

Gibson, J. P., and N. T. Wheelwright. "Genetic Structure in a Population of a Tropical Tree, *Ocotea tenera* (Lauraceae): Influence of Avian Seed Dispersal." *Oecologia* 103 (1995): 49–54.

Grime, J. P. "Evidence For the Existence of Three Primary Strategies in Plants and Its Relevance to Ecological and Evolutionary Theory." *American Naturalist* 111 (1977): 1169–1194.

Hare, R. C. "Contribution of Bark to Fire Resistance." *Journal of Forestry* 63 (1965): 248–251.

Harmon, M. "Fires in Great Smoky Mountains National Park." *Ecology* 65 (1984): 796–802.

Harper, J. L. *Population Biology of Plants.* San Diego, CA: Academic Press, 1987.

Herrera, C. M. "Seed Dispersal by Animals: A Role in Angiosperm Diversification?" *American Naturalist* 33 (1989): 309–322.

Hinrichsen, D. "A Human Thirst." In *Annual Editions: Environment 2004/2005.* Dubuque, IA: McGraw-Hill/Dushkin, 2004.

Hoffman, C. "Ecological Risks of Genetic Engineering of Crop Plants." *BioScience* 40 (1990): 434–437.

Howe, H. F., and L. C. Westley. *Ecological Relationships of Plants and Animals.* New York: Oxford University Press, 1988.

Keever, C. "Causes of Succession in Old Fields of the Piedmont, North Carolina." *Ecological Monographs* 20 (1050): 229–250.

Knapp, A. K., J. M. Blair, J. M. Briggs, S. L. Collins, D. C. Hartnett, L. C. Johnson, and E. G. Towne. "The Keystone Role of Bison in North American Tallgrass Prairie." *BioScience* 49 (1999): 39–50.

Lanner, R. M. "Adaptations of Whitebark Pine for Seed Dispersal by Clark's Nutcracker." *Canadian Journal of Forest Research* 12 (1982): 391–401.

Leopold, A. *A Sand County Almanac.* New York: Oxford University Press, 1949.

Levetin, E., and K. McMahon. *Plants and Society.* New York: WCB/McGraw-Hill, 1999.

MacArthur, R. H., and E. O. Wilson. *The Theory of Island Biogeography.* Princeton, NJ: Princeton University Press, 1967.

Matson, P. A., W. Parton, A. G. Power, and M. J. Swift. "Agricultural Intensification and Ecosystem Properties." *Science* 277 (1997): 504–509.

Mitton, J. B., and M. C. Grant. "Genetic Variation and the Natural History of Quaking Aspen." *BioScience* 46 (1996): 25–31.

Mollis, M. C. *Ecology Concepts and Applications.* New York: McGraw-Hill, 2002.

Mutel, C. F., and J. C. Emerick. *From Grassland to Glacier: The Natural History of Colorado and the Surrounding Region.* Boulder, CO: Johnson Books, 1992.

Nadkarni, N., and N. T. Wheelwright. *Monteverde: Ecology and Conservation of a Tropical Cloud Forest.* New York: Oxford University Press, 2000.

Odum, E. P., and G. W. Barrett. *Fundamentals of Ecology*, 5th ed. Belmont, CA: Thompson Brooks/Cole, 2005.

Osborn, F. *Our Plundered Planet.* Boston: Little, Brown, 1948.

Pitillo, J. D., R. D. Hatcher, Jr., and S. W. Buol. "Introduction to the Environment and Vegetation of the Southern Blue Ridge Province." *Castanea* 63 (1998): 202–216.

Pollan, M. *The Botany of Desire.* New York: Random House, 2001.

Quammen, D. *The Song of the Dodo: Island Biogeography in an Age of Extinctions.* New York: Touchstone, 1996.

Raven, P. H., G. Johnson, J. B. Losos, and S. R. Singer. *Biology*, 7th ed. New York: McGraw-Hill, 2005.

Regal, P. J. "Ecology and Evolution of Flowering Plant Dominance." *Science* 196 (1977): 622–629.

Richards, A. J. *Plant Breeding Systems.* London: George Allen and Unwin, 1986.

Schrader, J. A., and W. R. Graves. "Intraspecific Systematics of *Alnus maritima* (Betulaceae) from Three Widely Disjunct Provenances." *Castanea* 67 (2002): 380–401.

Bibliography

Schubert, S. D., M. J. Suarez, P. J. Pegion, R. D. Koster, and J. T. Bacmeister. "On the Cause of the 1930s Dust Bowl." *Science* 303 (2004): 1855–1859.

Shen-Miller, J., M. B. Mudgett, J. W. Schopf, S. Clarke, and R. Berger. "Exceptional Seed Longevity and Robust Growth: Ancient Sacred Lotus from China." *American Journal of Botany* 82 (1995): 1367–1380.

Shipley, L. A. "Grazers and Browsers: How Digestive Morphology Affects Diet Selection." In *Idaho Forest, Wildlife and Range Experimental Station Bulletin* #70 (1999): 20–27.

Smil, V. "Crop Residues: Agriculture's Largest Harvest." *BioScience* 49 (1999): 299–308.

Smith, R. L., and T. M. Smith. *Ecology and Field Biology.* Menlo Park, CA: Benjamin Cummings, 2001.

Snow, A. A., and P. M. Palma. "Commercialization of Transgenic Plants: Potential Ecological Risks." *BioScience* 47 (1997): 86–96.

Spurr, S. H., and B. V. Barnes. *Forest Ecology.* Malabar, FL: Krieger Publishing, 1992.

Townsend, C. R., J. L. Harper, and M. Begon. *Essentials of Ecology.* New York: Blackwell Science, 2000.

Uno, G., R. Storey, and R. Moore. *Principles of Botany.* New York: McGraw-Hill Higher Education, 2001.

Vaughan, D. A., and L. A. Sitch. "Gene Flow from the Jungle to Farmers." *BioScience* 41 (1991): 22–28.

Venable, D. L. "The Evolutionary Ecology of Seed Heteromorphism." *American Naturalist* 126 (1985): 577–595.

Vitousek, P. M., H. A. Mooney, J. Lubchenco, and J. M. Melillo. "Human Domination of Earth's Ecosystems." *Science* 277 (1997): 494–499.

Whittaker, R. H. *Communities and Ecosystems,* 2nd ed. London: Macmillan, 1975.

Whittaker, R. H., F. H. Boorman, G. E. Likens, and T.G. Siccama. "The Hubbard Brook Ecosystem Study: Forest Biomass and Production." *Ecological Monographs* 44 (1974): 233–252.

Wilson, E. O. "Biodiversity: Challenge, Science, Opportunity." *American Zoologist* 32 (1992): 1–7.

Wilson, E. O. *The Future of Life.* New York: Vintage Books, 2002.

Further Reading

Attenborough, D. *The Private Life of Plants.* Princeton, NJ: Princeton University Press, 1995.

Blackmore, S., and E. Tootill, eds. *The Facts on File Dictionary of Botany.* New York: Facts on File, 1984.

Devine, R. *Alien Invasion: America's Battle with Non-Native Animals and Plants.* Washington, DC: National Geographic, 1999.

Durrell, G. *A Practical Guide for the Amateur Naturalist.* London: Alfred A. Knopf, 1982.

Erickson, J. *A History of Life on Earth: Understanding Our Planet's Past.* New York: Facts on File, 1995.

Kleus, M. "The Big Bloom." *National Geographic* 202 (2002): 102–121.

Miller, G. T. *Essentials of Ecology.* Pacific Grove, CA: Brooks/Cole, 2005.

Montaigne, F. "No Room to Run." *National Geographic.* 204 (2004): 34–55.

Morell, V. "The Variety of Life." *National Geographic* 195 (1999): 6–31.

Morell, V. "Wilderness Headcount." *National Geographic* 195 (1999): 32–59.

Niklas, K. "What's So Special About Flowers?" *Natural History* 108 (1999): 42–45.

Young, P. *The Botany Coloring Book.* New York: Harper Collins, 1982.

Websites
Botanical Society of America
http://www.botany.org.

Bristlecone Pine
http://www.blueplanetbiomes.org/bristlecone_pine.htm

Eastern Native Tree Society
http://www.uark.edu/misc/ents/home.htm

Ecological Society of America
http://www.esa.org

Flora of North America
http://www.fna.org/FNA/

The Everglades Foundation
http://www.saveoureverglades.org/polluter/class/class_main.html

National Biological Information Infrastructure
http://www.nbii.gov/disciplines/botany/

National Interagency Fire Center Wildland Fire Statistics
http://www.nifc.gov/stats/wildlandfirestats.html

National Parks Portfolio
http://www.cr.nps.gov/history/online_books/portfolio/portfolio3b.htm

Rocky Mountain Tree Ring Research, Inc.
http://www.rmtrr.org

Royal Botanic Gardens, Kew
http://www.rbgkew.org.uk/

Smithsonian National Museum of Natural History
http://www.mnh.si.edu/

Ultimate Tree Ring Web Pages
http://web.utk.edu/~grissino/

U.S.D.A. PLANTS Database
plants.usda.gov.

U.S. Fish and Wildlife Service Threatened and Endangered Species System
http://ecos.fws.gov/tess_public/TESSWebpage

Wayne's Word Online Textbook of Natural History
http://waynesword.palomar.edu

Index

Index

Index

Picture Credits

J. Phil Gibson holds degrees in Botany from Oklahoma State University (B.S.) and the University of Georgia (M.S.), and Environmental Population and Organismic Biology from the University of Colorado (Ph.D.). He is currently Associate Professor and Chair of the Department of Biology and the Director of Environmental Studies at Agnes Scott College. His research investigates the ecology and evolution of plant reproductive systems. He also conducts conservation-focused research on tree species. He has published a variety of research papers and presented his work at scientific conferences. Gibson is a member of the Project Kaleidoscope Faculty for the 21st Century in recognition of his efforts to improve undergraduate science education. He is an active member of the Botanical Society of America and the Association of Southeastern Biologists.

Terri R. Gibson holds a degree in Zoology from the University of Georgia (B.S.). She has worked as a scientific illustrator and also as a research assistant studying, among other things, plant population genetics, plant morphology, and HIV. Currently, she is pursuing a career in children's literature.